THE
ENERGY
BOOK

THE
ENERGY
BOOK

Supercharge your life by
healing your energy

KALISA AUGUSTINE

POP PRESS

1 3 5 7 9 10 8 6 4 2

Published in 2020 by Pop Press an imprint of Ebury Publishing

20 Vauxhall Bridge Road,
London SW1V 2SA

Pop Press is part of the Penguin Random House group of companies
whose addresses can be found at global.penguinrandomhouse.com

Photo credits: page ii Mat Reding, Unsplash; v vovik_mar, istock; 12 sarawootch,
istock; 17 Babayev, istock; 18 m-gucci, istock; 21 kyoshino; 45 Victor_Tongdee,
istock; 62 dlinca, istock; 65 Kalisa Augustine; 77 kamisoka, istock; 88 littleny, istock;
94 SanneBerg, istock; 102 Kalisa Augustine; 116 tuncaycetin, istock; 135 Brunomili,
istock; 140 Ian Parker, Unsplash; 147 AnnaRise, istock; 156 kieferpix, istock;
166 Slavica, istock; 194 borchee, istock; 206 urbazon, istock;
209 GeorgeBurba, istock; 216 Kalisa Augustine.

Cover photo by undefined undefined, istock.

Illustrations © Suzanne Dias 2020 (with the exception of page 65 © Kalisa Augustine)

First published by Pop Press in 2020

www.penguin.co.uk

A CIP catalogue record for this book is available from the British Library

ISBN 978 1 529 10523 0

Colour origination by Rhapsody Ltd London
Printed and bound in China by Toppan Leefung

CONTENTS

FOR HELENA,
CHILD OF THE LIGHT

'We all have the extraordinary coded within us, waiting to be released.'

JEAN HOUSTON, WRITER, PHILOSOPHER AND THINKER

INTRODUCTION

Why did you pick up this book? Have you heard something about 'energy'?

I'm speaking of the force that makes you feel alive, vital and balanced. Not necessarily the kind that keeps the lights on or powers your car, but an inner kind. It fuels your experiences. It can help get you through a workout, make clear decisions, and enable you to feel connected to something greater or to attract the right kind of people into your world.

Are you newly awakened to certain psychic sensitivities or unexplainable synchronicities in your life and wondering what you can do to learn more? Perhaps you've tried or heard about some type of energy healing? Perhaps you have changed your perspective on how you want to approach spiritual life-questions? Do you ever feel other people's emotions and wonder if you are empathic? Maybe you've heard yoga teachers discuss energy and the power of intention?

Ever wondered where Reiki comes from and who can use it? Or whether you can mix it in with your own beliefs? You might go to acupuncture and not understand why it makes you feel so good. What's the big deal with affirmations? And what actually is the power of prayer?

What if you want to experience an energetic process that is not based on a specific religion or tradition, but helps you connect to your personal power? Perhaps you have come from a lineage rich in spiritual tradition and want to understand how to deepen the intimacy of your experience. We hear people talk about 'positive vibes' all the time, right? But what does that *actually* mean and why is it important in your everyday life?

In this book, we're going to take a look at what energy awareness is and why it's so vital. There are many versions of that explanation. Some have been around for thousands of years, some come from alternative health practitioners and others from world religions. You will probably already be aware that yoga traditions, martial arts, sports and even modern medicine incorporate an awareness of energy, but consciously practising energy healing techniques can offer you new wisdom. Put into practice, this wisdom can help create profound ways for you to change, heal and grow.

I have created this book to give you the power to meaningfully direct the path of your life by understanding yourself as an energy being. You are the boss. You can change your life for the better! You can create a more positive environment by harnessing the power of your inner light.

Let's get started…

'Yesterday I was clever, so I wanted to change the world. Today I am wise, so I am changing myself.'

RUMI, POET, SCHOLAR AND THEOLOGIAN

HOW TO USE THIS BOOK

The terrain of this book covers many different cultures, belief systems and spiritual practices, while highlighting their common threads. I will be discussing the key concepts behind each of these as they appear throughout the book. There are also further explanations, practices and meditations interwoven to help you implement these ideas. Once you've read the book through, you can then refer back to it as a guide to keep these ideas fresh, or dip into sections to focus on areas of special interest.

- **INTRODUCTION:** This part of the book is about *understanding energy* and will provide a foundational framework for what follows. It will illuminate these essential questions: Why energy? Why does it matter now? How do I relate to this? How does an energy process affect a situation?

- **1. HOW TO TUNE IN:** Part One is about *expansion* and is designed to guide you as you open up to new ideas. I have provided exercises that will help you expand beyond an awareness of your physical body and to cultivate non-traditional forms of intelligence. You will discover how unlocking your intuition and working with your energy can help you in so many different ways.

- **2. UNLOCK YOUR POWER:** Part Two is about *discovery* and will explore healing systems and particular areas of study that may align with you on your path. As you read this section, notice what lights you up. Explore and learn. Implement what resonates and continue your own research as you move forwards.

- **3. SUPERCHARGE YOUR LIFE:** Part Three is about *enhancing* your self-care and personal power by implementing these everyday practices to supercharge your life.

WHAT IS ENERGY?

People often ask me these questions: What is energy? What is energy healing? Why should I care about it?

My answer to the first question is:

Everything is energy.

You are an energy being.

Everything is born of patterns created by energy.

I try to respond to the second two questions by offering a greater context for how to integrate these concepts into our everyday lives so we can experience more joy and health. In my journey as a healer, I have become aware that many forms of healing are open to us. When I started, I was attracted to intuition-based approaches. Some were already familiar to me and others less so. As I became more aware of what I have to offer, I gravitated towards understandings that enhanced my inherent talents and branched out from there.

I was born with an intuitive sensibility. I've had to learn how to work with that and to manage it throughout my life. This is why I now lean towards an intuitive, shamanistic healing style that incorporates working with angels. I have indigenous *curanderas,* or Latin American shamans, in my family background, as well as Irish and Basque mystical lineages, so there may be some inherited instinct, which is why I find this work comes very easily to me. My inner artist enjoys working with colour, sound and feeling to create a unique experience, which is why I incorporate sound healing, chromotheraphy and therapeutic-grade crystals in my vibrational medicine practice. The Tudor philosopher Sir Thomas More once said, 'The soul has an absolute, unforgiving need for regular excursions into enchantment. It requires them like the body needs food and the mind needs thought.' I deeply resonate with this.

Other practitioners have wonderful approaches for tracking complex information by, for example, studying bodily systems or looking at neurological data as it relates to meditation. You might find that those sorts of approach speak to you and choose to build on that kind of knowledge base for your growth. We are all multi-faceted, unique human beings and have to understand where our strengths lie in order to grow.

How Do I Relate to This?

My own healing practice combines intuition, empowerment guidance, energy healing and vibrational medicine to elevate

'If you wish to understand the secrets of the Universe, think in terms of energy, frequency and vibration.'

NIKOLA TESLA, INVENTOR AND ENGINEER

my process. I talk about some of those aspects in this book, as well as other areas that have influenced my work. But I also want to give you a wide range of options to consider as you get started on your healing path. This way, you can feel what is right for you. Some are more scientifically based, as mentioned above, whereas other techniques are simply more accessible; some are ancient and some are combinations of old and new.

In the ancient Chinese philosophy of Taoism, qi (chi) is a Life-Force energy that is managed and cultivated through actions and awareness according to the practice of long-standing spiritual disciplines. In the acupuncture system, for instance, there are meridians or energy pathways that can be adjusted to improve the energy flow or balance. Indigenous peoples of many shamanic traditions believe that all things are alive and are possessed of Life Force; that Spirit is the substance behind matter, and when we have a harmonious connection with nature we can experience the benefits of that relationship. From plant medicine and spirit animals, to chromotherapy and yoga – this book provides an introduction to a variety of these approaches and techniques.

How Does Energy Influence a Situation?

Your energy follows your intention. Your vibe is your essence.
It is where your pure potential resides. It is your mojo. It speaks
for you before you even walk into a room. Once you get to
know yourself beyond the physical body, you may find a greater
sense of peace, health, joy, vitality and love. As you learn to
harness the power of your energy, you can unlock the ability
to create and attract the life conditions you desire. By working
internally, life changes externally. Since you are a harmonious
part of your environment, you can affect life around you by
making the commitment to thrive.

Thanks to quantum physics, we know that we are made up of
tiny, connective particles that vibrate at different frequencies.
Energetic vibrations are tangible, real and visible. The Universe
is full of energy. That power source is within us, just as we are
within it! It connects us all. Reaching our greatest potential is
achieved by harnessing this energy.

Healing is in part about holding and using higher awareness.
We all have an opportunity to use this higher awareness to
create health, wellbeing, clarity, success and joy. We can
use this understanding to overcome obstacles – no matter
who we are.

Expanding your awareness around energy helps to create harmony in all areas of life. The inner growth work that we human beings must go through as part of our journey on this planet is often about letting go and releasing patterns, obstacles and belief systems that affect your energy flow. How you manage your energy matters, and your consciousness opens the door, so 'break on through to the other side'.

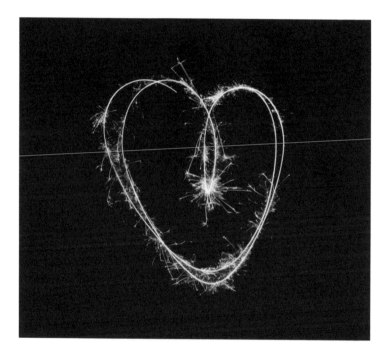

YOU ARE AN ENERGY BEING

Mystics believe there is sentience in each molecule. Even if you don't ascribe to that belief, there is a lot of complexity in the human body. You are made of trillions of cells. One cell can contain trillions of atoms. How did a single-celled fertilised egg know how to create you, your potential and consciousness? Random? I think not.

There is a benevolent, life-giving, creative field of intelligence that serves as the energetic component behind all things in the material world. Beyond form, there is essence — that same essence that connects us all. I will be referring to that field of intelligence, or essence, interchangeably throughout the book as the Source, Light or Spirit. There are many other names too for this Source: religious deities such as God, Great Spirit, Allah, Yahweh, Brahma, as well as the abstract energies of qi (chi) and prana. The list is endless, as are the interpretations of this essence.

My point is this: source energy is sentient. It knows what to do.

Understanding that there is an intelligent energy from which we are born is the basis for many mystical traditions. This understanding leads us to the idea that energy precedes all physical manifestation. In fact, according to some yogic traditions, the first energy centre, or chakra, to develop in the womb as the physical body is forming, is the solar plexus above the naval centre. Not only are we physical bodies, we are energy systems in development.

In Hinduism, the chakras are energy centres within and around the physical body that correlate to certain life areas, glands, organs and levels of vitality. In this tradition, just as your physical body forms in the womb, so does your energy body. The word 'chakra' originates from the Sanskrit word for 'wheel' or 'disc' and these energy centres are animated by prana, another word for Life-Force or Source energy. (We will be getting into chakras in more detail in Part One.) Buddhist lineages also acknowledge and incorporate understandings of the chakra system into their practices.

All living beings also have an energy field, which is sometimes described as an aura or electromagnetic field. This is the energy that exists around the physical body. It can be described as the condition and vibration of our energy in colour, frequency, light, patterns and density. Each person's aura is like a fingerprint. It is unique. The aura acts like the invisible representation of who you are and is intrinsically related to your physical wellbeing.

Your energy vibrates at different frequencies depending on where you are and what's going on in your world. Just as your physical body operates at different levels of health depending on how you treat it and your personal circumstances, your energy field is affected by how you treat it, too. How you handle life will create your energetic state. For instance, let's say you've just come home from an exhausting work trip. You see an email inviting you to go on a mini-break with a group of friends who often cause you to feel drained after spending time with them. (Have you ever had friends whose company can feel more like a chore than joy?) In this hypothetical scenario, spending more time with energies you find depleting when you are already exhausted from work is not a choice that honours your inner Light. Why? Because your energy field may need time to replenish and recover, just like your physical body does.

Replenishment comes from choosing conditions that power up your Light and energy. When we overextend our energy, pointing our focus towards aspects we find draining, we lose inner balance and leak Life-Force energy. When we honour our inner Light and support it through our behaviour, we amplify its power. Our vibration both influences the way we feel and our clarity around our lifestyle choices.

In other words: how you vibe is how you roll.

YOUR TIME IS NOW

Sometimes the world seems bleak, chaotic or hard to understand. We see injustice and destruction in the news every day. It makes sense that a sane person might feel occasional despair. However, seeing something you don't like doesn't necessarily mean you have to accept it as the way things are. If you feel as if you don't fit into the world, maybe you are meant to help change it? No matter how small or big the act, you have the power to make life better for yourself and those around you. And now is the time to make that choice.

There are cyclical patterns to observe and address on this planet, and we are in a highly transformational age. As the old adage suggests, it's a 'break down to break through' kind of moment. Though these times may create a sense of confusion, we also have a choice to evolve. These themes are discussed in the Hindu Vedas, some of the world's oldest sacred texts, written between roughly 1800 to 1000 BCE, as well as in Mayan and Hopi prophecies.

The ancient Hopi petroglyph on Prophecy Rock near Oraibi, Arizona speaks of the current age as 'purification days' and a rebirth of consciousness. The Age of Aquarius is the astrological period we are currently entering (see pages 144–145).

It signals a time of greater awareness, open communication, transparency and information, all at our fingertips. The rapid technological advancements and globalisation that come with this age make us constantly inundated with new information. *But guess what?* Doctors are telling us our nervous systems haven't caught up yet with these advances! We must learn to find balance. We must upgrade our perception and self-care practices during this period to stay centred. And it is my hope that this book will help you do just that!

Now, let's talk about how to tune into your vibe so you can roll like a boss...

1 . HOW TO TUNE IN

So here we are. We've acknowledged that some form of energy or Universal Life Force exists out there. But how do we really get started? Well, the first order of business is to become aware of the subtle energy within and around you. Just like in any relationship, you have to meet one another, get acquainted and hang out regularly to form and strengthen your connection. When you recognise yourself as an energy being and not just a cluster of thoughts and anxieties, it is easier to identify the energies around you. You'll be able to tell when something feels off, or, conversely, when a situation feels aligned.

To become better acquainted with yourself in this way, you need neutrality. This is a process of slowly emancipating your mind from old patterns of judgement. You begin to see life from a neutral vantage point in an environment of unprejudiced clarity. Neutrality is important because it creates space for truth to blossom within you without the noise and static of desires, anxieties, fears or illusions. These are thieves of peace and will cloud your sense of knowing. A regular stillness practice will help you cultivate neutrality and develop your awareness of energies. Working with visualisation, your breath and intention will deepen your understanding of yourself as an energy being.

GET TO KNOW YOUR ENERGY

Try this simple stillness practice at any time of the day. Whether you feel overwhelmed or vibrant, it's day or night, you're at work or at home, learning to use stillness and your breath as coping tools will help you to balance your body, mind, emotions and energy. These two focusing tools will help strengthen your meditation practice. (See also 'Meditation', pages 173 to 180.)

- Imagine breathing energy in the form of pure light into your heart centre and your lungs on your inhalation.

- Visualise the radiance filling your lungs and spreading out through your body.

- Allow yourself to relax all the other parts of your body as glistening Light fills your being from head to toe.

- You may start feeling the pulse of the heart in different locations. For example, in your naval point or behind your knees or in your hands.

- Allow this sense of full, pulsing radiance to act as the Life Force moving through you.

- Let all thoughts go. Each time you are distracted, return your focus to your breath of light. Stay with your inhalations and exhalations.

- Try this practice for 7 to 11 minutes at first, working up to longer sessions of about 20 minutes as you grow more comfortable with it.

DEVELOPING INTUITION

Do you ever feel like something in your life just doesn't sit right; it causes an uneasy feeling? Have you ever had multiple viable life pathways present themselves before you at the same time, each possibility paired with a healthy balance of pros and cons? On paper, maybe one option seems the most reasonable, but, deep down, you know it is time to take the road less travelled, even if it doesn't make sense quite yet. This is your intuition speaking (the word 'intuition' is from the Latin *intueri*, meaning 'to consider') and from a Western perspective, this is like trusting your gut. From an Eastern perspective, you could think of it as allowing your inner knowing to guide the way. Tuning in to your intuition is one of the easiest ways to get to know your energy. Your intuition is a powerful tool.

If you find yourself in a bind and don't know what to do, when the answers aren't in and time is running out — there is no need to waste hours, days or even weeks feeling tense and playing mental ping-pong in a desperate attempt to source solutions. Fear-based vibrations will source fear-based solutions. It is very important to feel and process our emotions; however, overindulging in anxiety on hyper-drive really doesn't serve anything or anyone. These are the moments where we really need our intuition to act as our north star, shining brightly when all is dark. If you spend time practising stillness and neutrality, it will be easier to call on your intuition when it really matters.

You might be wondering where to start, so that you can hear your intuition when it speaks to you. When too many ideas and concepts muddle your clarity, begin by taking your thoughts out of the equation. Listen to your body and energy instead. Your intuition and gut instincts communicate through these vessels.

To do this, you have to be patient while you cultivate a state of neutrality so that desires, overcharged emotions or fears don't distract you. To listen to your intuition clearly, you have to be grounded. Being grounded means feeling like you are connected, breathing freely and experiencing a sense of strength and peacefulness in your physical body. It means both your feet are planted firmly on the ground. Your mind is not jumping around at high speeds. You are not reacting. Instead, you are acting with intention.

VISUALISATION TO GROUND YOURSELF

Practise this exercise any time you like. It can stand alone
or be done alongside the previous exercise on page 22.
Alternatively, try it before or after your regular meditation
practice if you have one.

- Ideally find a quiet spot outside, perhaps in a park or in
  your garden. If a tree is available, sit comfortably under
  its shade or, even better, with your spine against the trunk.
  The older the tree, the better.

- If you live in an apartment in a big city, buy a potted plant
  that you can tend and nourish. For this exercise, sit next to
  your plant.

- Sit quietly with your eyes closed, breathing slowly in a
  steady rhythm.

- As you breathe, take your awareness to your feet.

- Next, move your awareness up to your ankles.

- Then on to your calves and lower legs.

- Slowly work up the body until you reach the top of your head.

- Set this intention internally, in your mind: *May all aspects of my whole self be fully integrated into my physical body.*

- Mentally affirm: *I am grounded in my physical body. My body is my temple and houses my energy. I honour my body and it honours me. Thank you, physical body, for telling me when I am moving too fast. We are allies. Thank you for teaching me how to listen.*

- If you are seated with your back against a tree, ask the tree to help ground you. Ask her roots to help you feel your depth. Ask her shade to protect you on your path. You will feel the tree's energy healing you.

- If you are in an apartment, ask the same of your potted plant.

- Feel gratitude as you honour the earth and the plant kingdoms.

- Continue breathing deeply into your core.

- Visualise filling your centre with light.

Once you've tuned in to your intuitive feelings and accepted them, the next step is to have the courage to act on what you know is right and aligned for your life. If a clear path is not yet visible, be patient and observant. Trust that the way will present itself when you are ready.

These kinds of ideas around patience and intentional non-action stem from Eastern philosophies like Zen Buddhism or Taoism, which is an ancient Chinese philosophy based on the writings of Lao Tzu. It is often very difficult for the Western mind to conceptualise and implement 'under-thinking it' and 'under-doing it', but it works. Keep it simple. Never make a decision on a high or a low. Intuition doesn't rush; it knows. Be patient enough to wait for true knowing.

Unlocking Your Intuition

I view intuition not as some magical, otherworldly power, but as the ability to use all of our expanded senses when navigating our way in life. This includes our instincts, which are often ignored. You can use your intuition and instincts to see situations more accurately and people for what they are, despite appearances. As you begin to activate your intuitive senses, combine these tools with your own deductive powers

'Muddy water
is best cleared by
leaving it alone.'

ALAN WATTS, PHILOSOPHER

of reasoning and logic. By doing so, you will gain access to a reliable, inner framework that helps you get to the truth of the matter.

As I mentioned above, to use your intuition effectively you must be calm, clear, balanced and feel centred. The goal is to create non-attachment to points of view, emotions or outcomes. Essentially, your personality takes a step back so you can access your intuition, allowing its insights to surface unimpeded.

Sometimes, we can be unconsciously biased. This is why cultivating neutrality is vital when working with intuition. Many people are unaware of their biases, which can create a stalemate in the conscious mind. In other words, while some people may believe they are enlightened, they can be totally off because they lack neutrality. When you approach life with integrity, seeking the best possible outcome for all involved and holding a genuine intention to be supportive and kind to both yourself and others, then you are not carrying divisiveness and negativity. You get more power, baby!

Challenge yourself by acquiring the discipline to strengthen your mind's 'neutral muscle'. To find your centre, begin by working with breath, meditation and visualisation, just as in the two exercises I've listed so far. Be willing to let go of what you think is supposed to happen. Imagine meditation and visualisation as being like the steering wheel of your car as you control its direction.

For example, if you find yourself stressed out with a racing mind after a conflict, take 10 minutes to yourself before reacting. Try 20 rounds of deep belly breathing, with your awareness focused on the flow of breath deep into your being – into your belly – while focusing on what it feels like in your physical body. In these moments, you can transcend your own preconceived notions.

There is no right or wrong, up or down, good or bad with a neutral, meditative mind. Instead, you are present and open. You accept what is. More often than not, the most profound insights and answers prove to be the most simple.

This all takes practice, but remember – practice makes perfect! With practice you can create the inner space for higher wisdom to drop in and direct you. Not only is this strategy more efficient, but it requires less effort and stress. The price however, is patience and trust. I'm thinking that's a fair trade.

I believe that intuition imbues us with the essence of divine wisdom. When these understandings land, you can use your

'The intuitive mind
is a sacred gift and
the rational mind
is a faithful servant.'

ALBERT EINSTEIN,
THEORETICAL PHYSICIST (ATTRIB.)

analytical or rational mind and personal will to make your hopes, dreams, goals or desired life-outcomes happen! The rational mind should serve the deeper, intuitive knowing, which stems from the heart. We need both to bring our dreams into reality. This brilliant mind we have is a powerful tool whose prime directive is to serve the path of the heart.

Let the heart lead and master your mind so you can use it wisely and strategically to build your heart's ultimate dream.

Intuition and the Heart

We cannot discuss intuition without understanding the magnitude of the power that is held in the heart centre. You don't have to be a Disney princess to listen to your heart! But understanding why the cliché exists at all will help you strengthen your connection to this centre, thus giving your intuitive senses a high-voltage boost.

We've already touched on the energy field known as the aura or electromagnetic field, which extends outwards in all directions from the physical body (see page 14). But did you know that the heart has its own micro-magnetic field within the energy body and that this is 100 times stronger than the brain's projected field? It also extends about 3 feet out of the body, according to the HeartMath Institute, a non-profit organisation that helps people reconnect with their heart.

From an energetic perspective, this information really gives you a glimpse into the power of the heart. When the heart chakra (the energy centre associated with the heart) is open, we have an opportunity to develop a new relationship with our feelings. This energy centre represents our capacity to give and receive love. It is the chief intuitive sensory centre for the entire body, and the golden gateway to making conscious contact to Spirit.

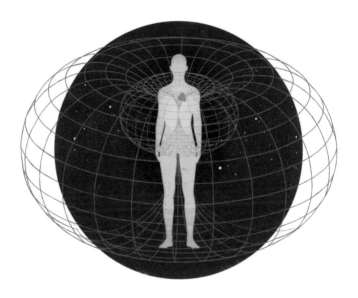

The structure of the auric field, with the heart's field contained within it.

This centre is associated not only with love but also spiritual awakening, because you cannot activate one without activating the other. It also governs boundaries and the immune system. The heart will tell you when something is off or when a relationship is out of balance. The heart is also the balancing point in the body between the body's lower energy centres (or chakras) and its upper energy centres – sort of like a metaphorical link between heaven and earth.

We know when someone is speaking from their heart because heartfelt communication touches the soul. In fact, any idea, creation, word or thought stemming from an open source of love in the heart, with its strong connection to the divine, will have healing powers.

However, sometimes – as with the body's other energy centres – this centre can get out of balance. When the heart centre is overactive, for example, a person may be subject to an overdeveloped sense of sympathy. If the heart centre is underactive, they could have dependency issues or lose their sense of self.

If life gets muddled or unclear, when the path seems confused and wandering, do nothing – be still, and open your heart. Without the awareness afforded by the heart, we are lost. We simply cannot bypass the heart on the path to health and peace.

MEDITATION TO OPEN
THE HEART CENTRE

If you feel your heart is closed and there is no flow of love,
try this seated yet moving meditation for 7 to 31 minutes.
It uses a mantra, which is a word or sound that is repeated
to help you focus during the meditation.

- Sit on the ground with your legs crossed, with each
  foot tucked under the opposite knee and with a straight
  spine. If you are familiar with yoga, this is Easy Pose
  (Sukhasana).

- Lift your chest and sternum upwards while gently
  stretching the back of the neck by pulling the chin down.

- Keep your head level and centred, without tilting
  forwards or backwards or side to side.

- Let the muscles of your throat and neck relax.

- Let your face relax.

- With your eyes closed, look up and focus on the
  brow point.

- The mantra for this meditation is *Sat Kartaar*: *Sat* means essence of truth or being, while *Kartaar* means 'doer' or 'manifestor'. Combined together, the mantra means 'Walker of Truth'.

- As you say *Sat*, press your hands together in prayer pose at the centre of the chest.

- As you say *Kar*, extend your hands out from your shoulders, halfway towards the final position. Fingers are pointing straight up.

- As you say *Taar*, fully extend your arms out from the sides parallel to the floor, fingers still pointing up.

- Make the transition from step to step with flowing movements, and repeat until you are ready to end the meditation.

Intuition and Consciousness

When we live in harmony with our highest potential and true
selves, we will more easily be able to enter a state of flow
with life. When we have more clarity about who we really
are, there is greater opportunity for us to develop a form of
consciousness that embodies the ultimate truth, or Source
energy. This is known as unity consciousness, although it is
called by many other names in different cultures. Buddhists
may refer to it as 'nirvana'. Christians might experience this as
being aligned with the 'Holy Spirit'. A Zen practitioner may
be seeking a sense of 'emptiness'. The point is to develop a
practice that can help you connect with both your potential and
your True Self (also known as your Higher Self), and thereby
deepen your experience of life.

Many of us are often unable to identify the source of an inner
tension that blocks clarity; so get to know yourself. Knowing your
True Self will help you get to the root cause of any disharmonious
experience. And if you are reading this wondering, 'What if
I don't even know who I am?', worry not. Admitting that you
don't know who you are can act as a profound revelation that
marks the beginning of your spiritual journey. When you are a
little further down the path, by applying practically the insights

revealed to you through your intuition, open heart and clarity, you will bring a sense of wholeness to your life.

Wholeness comes from understanding yourself to be an energy being or a spiritual being that is having a physical experience. This knowing leads to a deep sense of inner autonomy. Instead of looking outside yourself for answers, you turn *inwards*. When you honour your highest truth and needs, you honour those around you with your truth. You set an example.

It takes courage to challenge yourself, to transcend the status quo and act on your own clarity. Yet innovation comes from *not* following old ways of thinking. So, where is inspiration born if not by looking at the way everyone else is doing things? That's right: by acting on your inner clarity and intuition, which is how your thoughts will evolve.

By tapping into your intuition you will be able to access new ways of being, thinking, seeing, creating and understanding the world. Game changers, pioneers and innovators tend to be highly attuned to their intuition. You are your own inner guru. That which you seek is yourself.

Do You Expand or Contract?

As an ongoing practice, begin to notice when you feel a
sense of expansion or contraction around certain people,
energies or life circumstances. Are there certain situations
where your physical body tenses up or relaxes? For
example, a sudden shift in body language, like slumping
your shoulders every time you are with a particular
person, may be indicative of a need to subconsciously
protect the heart, which could mean you don't feel fully,
emotionally safe with that individual. This would be a
type of contraction.

As you begin to notice where you open or close up
as you walk through the world, you can develop and
sharpen this sense and use it to listen to your internal
guidance. As you do so, the connection gets stronger.
This can be a subtle practice done at any time.
Consistency and regularity will strengthen it.

When you start deepening your intuition, you are able to harness more personal power. You won't feel threatened or as easily offended by chaos and discord because you stand tall, walking the world with your own road map.

The Intuitive Energy Centre

The 'third eye' is a common name for the energy centre, or chakra, located between and just above the eyebrows. This is the perceiver of intuition. In a yogic practice, it is called the *Ajna* centre. When open and attuned, the third eye is a neutral witness that allows us to see beyond the physical, beyond the present time, beyond our five senses and beyond our mind's understanding in the moment.

When we clear the third eye, this allows us to incorporate non-linear awareness into our understanding. Non-linear awareness is knowledge that extends beyond the perception of our five senses. It is non-binary and bigger than what we perceive around us. This kind of extra-sensory information is sourced from your intuition, your subconscious and your dream states, offering concepts and visions outside of your normal stream of awareness.

We all have access to deeper, unconstrained awareness. Some people are visual and will receive this knowledge in the form of images, while others will hear or 'feel' the information. Some people receive a combination coming from different senses.

We can now see how important it is to be open and clear to optimise our perception.

ACTIVATING THE THIRD EYE

You will need: a small amethyst crystal (optional) and a collection of other crystals to form a grid, pen and paper, metal bowl, box of matches.

This exercise is designed to open and clear the psychic centre of your energy body, your third eye. The first part of the exercise activates the third eye and creates a link between your Higher Self (the awakened aspects of your inner being that connects with the Source) and intuitive ability. The second part offers clearing steps, which bring together meditation, focus, intention and light energy, and which will help you remove any denser vibrations obscuring the lens of your higher vision.

Please do this exercise when you are feeling calm and centred. You may want some time to rest afterwards, so make sure you do this on a day where there is some flexibility in your schedule. This ritual is spiritually creative in nature. Read through all the steps first, then have fun with it!

The Opening Steps

- Close your eyes and take 8 long, slow and steady deep breaths.

- Make your exhales longer than your inhales.

- Visualise breathing in brilliant, golden light.

- Send that light to every part of your body.

- Mentally ask your third eye to awaken. (If you have a small amethyst crystal, place it over your third eye chakra if laying down, or place it in your left palm if sitting upright – see page 101 for more on amethyst.)

- Tell this energy centre you would now like to work together as its ally.

- Continue breathing consciously and raise up your hands with both palms facing forwards. (Carry on holding the crystal, if you have one in your hand.)

- Imagine that there is a sphere of light floating before you that is about the same size as your body.

- Imagine this is your truest, spiritual self – your Higher Self – containing the wisdom of the Universe.

- Feel the unconditional love this Light has to offer you.

- Feel the kindness and love envelop you.

- Ask the light to animate your inner wisdom.

- Imagine releasing fears and anxieties through your breath. Imagine breathing in clarity and truth for a few minutes.

- Thank your Higher Self and open your eyes.

The Clearing Steps

- Close your eyes and meditate for a few minutes on filling your entire body and energy field with light.

- Begin clearing by visualising blue energy being pulled through both thumbs as you inhale. Feel this blue energy running up your arms, into your temples, with both streams meeting at the third eye.

- As you exhale, visualise the blue light moving outwards through the middle of your forehead.

- Repeat this with your index finger, middle finger, ring and little finger.

- Repeat this 5 times with your palms.

- Then visualise drawing in streams of white light through both palms into your temples as you inhale, and release the energy through the centre of your forehead on the exhale. Repeat this 5 times.

- Open your eyes when you are finished.

- Take your pen and paper and, on separate pieces of paper, write down the areas where you feel blocked, stagnated or otherwise foggy and unclear. Keep them as short and clear as possible, for example, 'Brain Fog' or 'Tired Mind' or 'Forgetful'.

- Set up a small grid of crystals and place a metal bowl in the middle. Using your intuition, arrange the crystals while holding the intention to clear the third eye as you make this sacred grid. (The grid often resembles a crystal mandala, but use your own intuition to create it.)

- Now take the papers with the issues and put them in the metal bowl. Light a match and burn the blockages you have written down as a symbol of the mind clearing these obstacles. You are instructing your subconscious with this process.

- When the burning ritual is complete, imagine summoning the Earth's energy up from the soles of your feet and in through your palms. This energy moves from your hands and feet into the third eye as you inhale. As you exhale, move the energy up through the top of the head and out through the crown.

- Complete the process by meditating in silence for a few minutes, eyes closed.

NOTE: This entire process should take 20 minutes.

Trust is needed to develop your intuition. Don't editorialise each step in the process, which would stop the flow of the experience. We must allow time to synthesise without the burden of simultaneously trying to analyse. It's OK if you don't understand everything at first. Give yourself some time to absorb it all. This is a part of what it means to be trusting.

You must develop your own 'intuition language' and build that vocabulary based on your experiences. You can practise using your intuition with things as simple as finding a parking spot or getting a sense of what foods will nourish your body during the course of the day. We'll work on developing our intuition further with the powerful practice of meditation later in this book (see pages 173–180).

UNDERSTANDING YOUR ENERGY FIELD

Being able to sense the energy around you and observing how
you naturally react to external, energetic conditions can provide
an advantage as you move through life. I bet you'd rather
know after a couple of dates that your crush lacks the emotional
sophistication required to meet your heart's needs, rather than
six months down the road? Interpreting energy with discernment
and wisdom helps you understand people and where they are in
their personal growth. You can use this intuitive sensory system to
decide what job to take, where to live, which friends really have
your back, how to handle a financial investment or even how to
approach a conflict at work.

Have you ever experienced this scenario? You're at a party
and having a good time, when all of a sudden, someone walks
in the room and zaps the mood. You feel uncomfortable, as
if something is off, despite having no background information
about this stranger. Your body tenses in the most subtle way, as
if it is constricting to protect itself. That is your inner knowing
conveying the quality of the vibrations around you to your
conscious mind, using your physical body and emotions as
communication vehicles.

Or perhaps you meet someone and, though you don't know why, you feel like you've just clicked! You're so on the same wavelength and it's almost spooky. It is as if you've known this person for years. The conversation is easy and smooth. You feel like yourself, totally at home, and your physical body relaxes.

What is actually happening here? Well, your energy fields are talking. And faster than the mental body can conceptualise and make decisions, your electromagnetic field is downloading and interpreting real data, or 'truth information', suggesting this new person is totally, freaking cool. But what do I mean when I say 'truth information'?

Energy Doesn't Lie

Lips can talk. Eyes can hide. But vibes don't lie.

People can say pretty things and put on airs, but it's a lot harder to be phony in front of someone who 'speaks' frequency because... energy doesn't lie.

The above-mentioned scenarios of someone entering a room or going on a date are just two examples of this, but when you become attuned to your True Self, it will be easier to sense what is uniquely aligned for you or not, without judgement. When you know yourself on an energetic level, you'll know if a person, place or situation is resonating with you. It's not about reading into anyone else's secrets or prying into someone else's life, but feeling where life is opening for you that can help guide you towards better choices. When you approach life with neutrality, you can use your feeling, senses and instincts to detect when something is off. You begin to learn your being's own unique system of signs and signals.

When you listen to your body, feelings, senses and instincts, you'll never again have to ask one of your friends whether you should go on a date with this person or not. You'll know by the way you read the energy whether it's a yes!

You could even do this when picking out a crystal to buy or work with. Just use your intuition and you'll know. You'll just feel it when browsing over stones in a shop. One will call out to you because you'll sense there is healing or positivity emanating from the crystal that can in some way help you. You don't have to know what kind of crystal it is, or how it helps. Of course, you can research and identify its properties all you want, and that information may be of service, but next time you're at a crystal shop, just choose the one that is calling to you without research or asking someone for help. Feel. Know. Choose. Go. Try it out!

Shine your Light on a Stranger

Here is a fun game to play when you've got a night out with your crew. The next time you go to a restaurant with your friends, use your energy and intuition to pick out who you are going to have the best chemistry with, of all the strangers in the place. There will be a moment when you zero in on someone and make your choice. But how did you make that choice?

It's not just about the way they look. It's not only about the way they dress. There's something else going on here. It's their energy, their swagger, their mojo. They've got the amps for you. Swagger has to do with energy and the way someone rolls. It's about their vibe.

All I'm asking you to do is pay more attention to the subtle energy available to you as you live your day-to-day life.

Have you ever heard someone say, 'Man, she can really read a room'? In essence, sensing subtle energy is being able to read the room. Except 'the room' is anywhere you are. And 'reading' means understanding energy. And guess what, if you can read the room, you can work the room. And this is where intuition helps empower you out in the world and enhance your success.

A simple way to start intuitively sensing energy is to watch what makes you expand and what makes you contract, as we've already seen. However, I am not asking you to stay in a place of reactivity, but observance. It's a very subtle awareness.

You may start spotting patterns that can offer clarity. What lights you up? Where do you feel alive and at ease? Who makes you feel like anything is possible? Becoming aware of these types of sensory indicators can expand your consciousness by providing insight and potentially helping you to create new patterns of self-honouring behaviour. Knowing what's good for you will up your self-care game. After all, how can you treat yourself well if you don't know what's beneficial to you in the first place? That is why I invite you to slow down and start paying attention to the energies around you.

Eventually you may get to the place where you are choosing to be a torch bearer; a beacon of light wherever you go because you've made up your mind to do so first thing upon rising. I can't tell you how many frustrating subway rides I've taken during rush hour in New York City, exhausted after work. But instead of feeling overwhelmed by vibrations I cannot control, I've made it a practice to visualise using my energy to fill the subway car with light. I play energy games by sending light to children in strollers as I smile at them with kindness.

If you find yourself in a stressful situation, try sending out light to the people around you and watch what happens. Sensing energy can be likened to something as simple as gently dipping your hand into a serene lake on a warm, summer evening and deciding if the water is the right temperature for you to take a swim. As you start opening your awareness, keep the process simple. Don't overthink it. Just watch what invigorates you as you move through your day and ask yourself: does this make me feel good?

7-DAY SENSING EXERCISE:
WHAT LIGHTS ME UP?

Here is a simple practice to help you understand your personal energy field and the things that resonate with it.

- Buy a small, pocket-sized journal or notebook and keep it in your bag or backpack.

- From morning to evening, write down anything that makes you feel uplifted or expanded (a sign of positive energy and the Life Force being present).

- Write down the details of the exact moment, conditions and catalyst that caused you to feel open and light-hearted.

- After one week, see if you notice any patterns or similarities in your notes.

- When complete, bless the moments and thank the Universe for them.

- Finally, thank your Higher Self in advance for sending you more opportunities to feel uplifted and peaceful.

WORKING WITH YOUR ENERGY FIELD AT HOME

Now that you've had some practice in sensing vibrations, it's time to start working with your own energy field at home. As we've already seen, energy patterns create the physical world. Remember, energy precedes all physical manifestation, and having a vibrant, flowing energy field helps to create a strong, clear connection to your intuition and its guidance.

Whenever we are in positions that entail giving away personal power, our energy field weakens. We lose power when we dishonour our spirit or True Self. So how does this happen? Well, by saying yes when you want to say no and suppressing your voice. You can also dishonour your spirit by engaging in toxic or abusive relationships, working in a job that you hate, engaging in drug and alcohol abuse or staying stuck in prolonged periods of grief, despair, depression, anxiety, anger, jealousy or other emotional states that affect your sense of centredness. You also lose power when you have a low sense of self-worth.

Are you a people-pleaser? People-pleasers aren't completely honest with themselves or others. They will bend over backwards to avoid confrontation or conflict – even at the expense of healing and truth. People-pleasing causes us to leak Life-Force energy. Lacking healthy boundaries depletes your energy field because you allow, consciously or not, other people to take advantage of your time, energy, money and ideas.

In the same way, traumas or physical accidents can jolt the energy system. Our field weakens by retracting closer into the physical body and sometimes tears or ruptures are created. In these states, you may become potentially more open to absorbing stuff that doesn't belong to you. It's like holding on to unnecessary weight that makes you feel heavy.

Energetic imbalances can create or exacerbate all sorts of pre-existing conditions: physical disharmony, anxiety, stress, addiction, headaches, jaw clenching, weight gain, weight loss, insomnia, financial problems, imbalanced emotional responses, relationship issues, depression, the inability to experience the synchronicity of life, fatigue (physical, mental or emotional), brain fog, dissociative behaviours, nightmares and creative blocks; and they can also inhibit your ability to heal fully from traumas. They can cause a lack of direction and purpose. These kinds of imbalances can affect the way you look, feel and speak.

When we go against what we instinctually know is the right life path, we lose Life Force, or prana. It is that simple. You cannot suppress who you truly are, and still expect to be a powerhouse. Energy healing is like a cosmic reboot that restarts your whole being with a sense of lightness and elevated vision. The practical benefits of a strong energy field include feeling lighter and alive, clarity of thought, emotional release, sound sleep, elevated energy levels, decreased depression and anxiety, a radiant glow, spiritual transformation, more easily entering states of flow and harnessing wisdom.

Energy is the cause. Your outer world is the effect.

As we have seen, we have energy centres within and around us, and layers of energy that extend outwards from the physical body. Many traditions around the world call these layers by different names and will break down the energy field according to their particular philosophy. For our purposes, simply understand that each layer is connected to the next as it extends outwards. For example, the outer layer of the auric field is also present within the first layer. And each layer corresponds to certain aspects of your being, such as your mental state, emotions, physical body, spiritual self, personal will and so on.

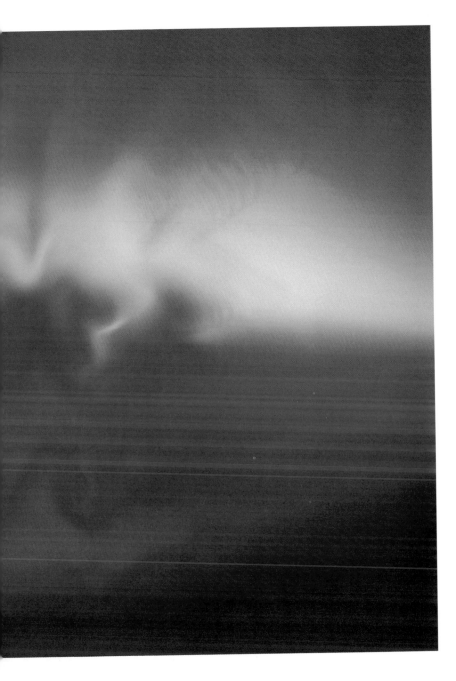

Your Primary Energy Centres – the Chakras

The seven primary energy centres, or chakras as described by the yogic system, are used in many energy healing practices today. People who practise energy healing and who do not practise yoga at all still use this system to assess the quality and vibrancy of a person's energy. The issue is that, like acupuncture systems and many other realms of healing, the chakras do not show up in scientific scans and are considered etheric energy structures. In other words, it is up to the practitioner to evaluate them intuitively – and that evaluation cannot be confirmed directly by medical practice.

So far we've only looked at the heart chakra in any detail; however, current understanding suggests that there are as many as 189 chakras in the human energy system. For our purposes, we are going to focus on the main seven. Again, these are vortices of energy in and around the body that correspond to areas of life and anatomical components, including organs and glands.

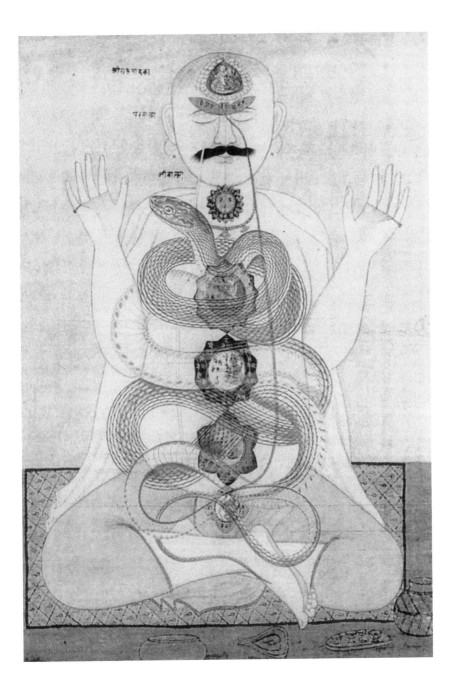

ROOT

Sanskrit Name: Muladhara (Mul = base, adhara = support)

Colour: red

Role: grounding and security

Objective: stability, safety, rootedness, self-preservation, feeling safe and secure, balanced, centred, decisiveness

Location: perineum, base of the spine

Physical Association: bones, legs, feet, base

Gland: adrenals

Gemstone: hematite, bloodstone, red garnet, red jasper, tourmaline

When the root chakra is healthy, flowing and vibrant, you will feel physically healthy with lots of vital energy, centred and strong, grounded and abundant. You will be decisive and clear.

SACRAL

Sanskrit Name: Svadhisthana (sva = self or prana, dhisthana = dwelling place)

Colour: orange

Role: relationships, creativity, emotions

Objective: sensual empowerment, reproduction, creative expansion, innocence, inspiration, desire, intimacy and letting go, feeling alive, sexual, warmth, affection, playfulness

Location: just below the naval

Physical Association: sex organs, large intestine, appendix, lower vertebrae, hips, spleen, urinary tract, ovaries, uterus

Gland: gonads

Gemstone: coral, carnelian

When this energy centre has good flow, the person will be stable, emotionally balanced and have a healthy sexual drive, while understanding how to set self-honouring boundaries in all forms of relationships. With a balanced sacral chakra, you will be able to use your creative force constructively – whether that means building a business, finishing a book or painting or having a child. You are playful and open to new ideas.

SOLAR PLEXUS

Sanskrit Name: Manipura (mani = jewel, pura = city)

Colour: yellow

Role: energy, vitality, ambition, digestion, Life Force distribution centre, self-assertion

Objective: willpower, personal authority, inner strength, self-control, purpose, vital energy, instinct, passion, anger, self-worth, manifestation, confidence, efficiency, perfectionism, control issues, courage, wisdom, physical strength, centredness

Location: area between the lower rib cage and naval

Physical Association: stomach, abdomen, liver, gall bladder, spleen, middle spine, digestive system, nervous system

Gland: pancreas, adrenals

Gemstone: amber, citrine, heliodor

When this energy centre is flowing and glowing, you will be productive, energetic, joyful, confident, cooperative, flexible, focused, empowered and successful.

HEART

Sanskrit Name: Anahata (unstruck or unbeaten)

Colour: green (front) and pink (back)

Role: love, compassion, intuition, hope

Objective: self-love and loving others in balance, sharing, warmth, forgiveness, connecting to Spirit, love, trust, flexibility, acceptance, spiritual growth, grief, tolerance, patience, kindness, radiance, balance, gratitude, intuition, intelligence

Location: heart

Physical Association: heart, circulatory system, immune system, lungs, blood, allergies, circulation

Gland: thymus

Gemstone: green tourmaline, kunzite, jade, rose quartz, Lemurian crystal

When this chakra is balanced, a person will be in love with life around them and have high self-esteem. They will be patient and kind, and less likely to take offence or give offence. Their ability to give and receive love and follow internal guidance is powerful. A healthy heart chakra equals a person with BIG LOVE.

THROAT

Sanskrit Name: Vishuddha (shuddi = to purify)

Colour: blue

Role: communication, speech, healing

Objective: creative expression, articulation, sharing truth from the heart, release, communion, communication, empowerment, openness, integrity, truthfulness

Location: throat

Physical Association: throat and neck, ears, sinus, respiratory system

Gland: parathyroid glands, thyroid

Gemstone: turquoise, azurite, blue celestite, blue chalcedony, aquamarine

When this energy centre is balanced, the person will find it easy to express their truth with eloquence and honesty, and be a good listener. In essence, you have the wisdom to know when to speak and when to remain silent. Expression will be like breathing, it is so natural. People are easily able to understand you and feel comfortable around you.

THIRD EYE

Sanskrit Name: Ajna (command post)

Colour: indigo

Role: intuition and psychic understanding, psychological health

Objective: seeing truth, using imagination to manifest, clarity, wisdom, divine insight, seeing the big picture, imaginative, service oriented, being focused on goodness, visionary

Location: slightly elevated point between the brows

Physical Associations: autonomic nervous system, eyes, brain

Gland: pituitary, pineal

Gemstone: lapis, amethyst, labradorite, blue sapphire

When the Ajna centre is healthy and balanced, the person will display intelligence and a clear head. They will be alert and thoughtful with a keen intuitive ability. They will be very wise and have a good memory, while being able to 'read between the lines'.

CROWN

Sanskrit Name: Sahasrara (thousand-petal lotus)

Colour: violet

Role: spiritual communion, enlightenment, transcendence

Objective: wisdom, higher consciousness, divine embodiment, oneness, divinity, higher values, cosmic love, compassion, harmony, peace, presence

Location: top of the head

Physical Associations: metabolism, nervous system, circadian rhythms, skin, bones, muscles, cerebral cortex, upper spine, hair

Gland: pineal

Gemstone: clear quartz, amethyst, lepidolite

With a healthy, flowing crown chakra, you can connect to a higher power within yourself and bring that awareness into your everyday life with finesse and an integrated balance. You are grounded and spiritual. You enjoy life without fearing death. You remain detached and neutral while compassionate and loving. You regularly connect with divine guidance to make good decisions.

Working on the Unconscious

So much of our mind and body is governed by aspects that we will never see or fully understand. Your unconscious self is vast. Thousands of operations and activities are going on in it every moment, from the regeneration of cells to the production of pancreatic fluids, to the unknown manipulations of the mind. The same goes for our energy. What we *can* do is use our available consciousness to improve our wellbeing.

Visualisations, meditations and energy interactions of all types affect us in countless ways. So why not take the bull by the horns and implement your own process to positively influence your energy and vitality in life?

When I feel out of flow, the first thing I do is balance and then clear my energy. Why? If I am in a situation I wish to change, I want to have all my best resources available to me. I want my clarity, my balance, my mental capacity and vitality to all be on point. I don't want any extra bullsh%t affecting my decision-making. It's a little bit like cleaning the house to help find your missing keys. A good way to start practising this for yourself is through visualisation techniques.

CHAKRA BALANCING VISUALISATION

As I've mentioned, each chakra centre corresponds to particular life areas and emotions, as well as physical body functions. You can learn to balance them with a simple process.

This simple visualisation can be done any time of day or night and should just take a few minutes.

In this practice, first set the intention for Spirit to help you balance the chakras. Then, try taking a few minutes to visualise the colours represented by each chakra in your mind's eye, letting each colour fill up your entire energy field in turn. As you do so, mentally affirm positive statements that address the functionality of the individual centre.

To begin, find a comfortable position and breathe deeply. Close your eyes to help yourself visualise each colour filling you up.

- **ROOT CHAKRA**: fill your mind's eye with a beautiful, cherry red to represent the root chakra as you silently say to yourself: *I am safe and secure.*

- **SACRAL CHAKRA**: use a clementine orange for the sacral chakra as you state: *I am inspired and creative.*

- **SOLAR PLEXUS CHAKRA**: use golden yellow, like a beautiful sunset, for the solar plexus as you say: *I stand confidently in my power.*

- **HEART CHAKRA**: emerald green works on the heart chakra while you affirm: *I am compassionate. I easily give love. I easily receive love. My heart is open. I am love.*

- **THROAT CHAKRA**: use sky blue for the throat chakra and say: *I express my truth easily and eloquently.*

- **THIRD EYE CHAKRA**: the third eye is represented by the colour indigo. Visualise indigo filling up your energy field while you tell yourself and the Universe: *I see divine truth.*

- **CROWN CHAKRA**: finally, visualise violet filling your imagination to represent the crown chakra as you say: *I am one with divine truth.*

Clearing Your Energy Field

We all have highs and lows. We all have to deal with the full spectrum of the human condition. Intellectual awareness of a particular pathology isn't enough to change the condition. What I mean by that is knowing you have a problem doesn't make it go away. However, creating new conditions in the present may put you on the path to affect change. Lifting away the dense energy that holds you back can really open the door to releasing your potential. Healthy emotional processing, caring for your physical body with diligence and training your mind towards neutrality and positivity, must accompany energetic self-care for the holistic approach to work long-term. And trust me, it will.

A clear energy field will enhance your ability to gracefully and efficiently manage your personal growth, healing process and conscious evolution. Energy healing will help to keep your process on course. When you let light in, you bring what is dark and hidden to the surface to be released. Doing so may cause you to feel lighter and understand your experience with greater wisdom.

To round off this part of the book, I'd like to share some of my favourite exercises for working with energy at home.

When ease settles in, life eases up.

A PRACTICE TO START THE DAY

Don't just jolt out of bed after the alarm clock goes off. When you arise from sleep, the realm of the deep unconscious mind is still close to your awareness. Give yourself a moment of calm before you are drawn into the busy world and your senses begin to tackle the logistics of the day ahead.

All you need is to take 12 to 14 minutes to integrate the wisdom of your dream time to your recently awakened state. The conscious meets the subconscious; sleeping meets waking, and this momentary marriage gives you the benefits of both to use in your day.

- Sit in a comfortable position or remain laying down in bed and close your eyes.

- Give thanks for the blessings of sleep and dream time.

- Ask your subconscious mind to bring forth wisdom gained from the past night. You don't have to know exactly what that is; simply set the intention and allow your Higher Self to integrate the wisdom on your behalf.

- Imagine sending the energy of this morning peacefulness into the rest of your day.

- After some time, use your breath and intention to let go of dream awareness and invite a focused, energised mentality to work with you as an ally.

- To complete the process, visualise two full breaths energising each chakra with light, working from the root chakra all the way up to the crown.

- Ask the Universe to take away any negative energy or dense vibrations that do not serve you. Imagine a blue tube of light like a vacuum absorbing any density or stagnation.

- Choose a poem or some conscious reading material to initiate your mindset for the day.

- Remain silent for 1 to 2 minutes before you rise and read the poem or piece of prose.

BILATERAL BREATHING

The purpose of this next exercise is to balance the left and right centres of the brain and to sharpen the mind. By using a technique that moves the brain's focus back and forth between its two hemispheres, the workings of the left and right brain begin to integrate more efficiently. This exercise can be done at any time of day, as required. This visualisation also relaxes the body and creates a restful yet aware state of mind.

This practice is broken up into two parts. After part A, allow the energy to circulate and assimilate for a few minutes, then move on to part B. The break between steps deepens the experience.

Part A

- Lay on your back with closed eyes.

- With your first inhale, visualise breathing in light from the bottom of your left foot.

- See this light travelling up to the heart.

- On the exhale, the light crosses over your right shoulder and down the arm, before releasing from your right palm.

- On the second inhale, draw light energy up from your right foot and again feel it travelling to your heart.

- As you exhale again, the light crosses over your left shoulder and down the arm, with light releasing from your left palm.

- This completes one cycle of the exercise.

- Now complete 12 cycles and take a short rest afterwards.

NOTES: *The inhale and exhale should be the same length and effort. The breath should not be rigorous. No hyperventilating should occur. The body should relax. A sensation of spaciousness will likely occur.*

Part B

- After the completion of 12 cycles in Part A, breathe in light up through both feet.

- Visualise this light moving into the heart.

- As you exhale, release the light through the crown of your head.

- Do this for 7 cycles and then rest peacefully for 3 to 5 minutes.

EXPANDING THE LIGHT FIELD

The purpose of this exercise is to bring more light into your energy field and to feel it expand. Part A generates the energy required and creates the environment needed to complete Part B.

Part A

- Lie down in a relaxed position with your eyes closed.

- Breathe light energy into the heart and lungs. Each inhale increases the amount of light and vitality in the body until the body becomes filled with light from head to toe.

- Visualise a spherical energy field emanating from your body.

- Focus on the sensations in your feet. Notice if there is a difference in the energy between your left and right foot... If there is, ask the light you've created to balance the feet.

- Repeat this process for the ankles, shins, knees, thighs, hips and solar plexus.

- Now move on to the hands, forearms, elbows, shoulders, heart, throat centre, forehead and crown of head.

NOTES: *If any emotions occur that distract you, continue to breathe those emotions up and out of the body effortlessly. If distracting thoughts occur, do the same thing. Your task is to not be distracted by thoughts or emotions. Your only purpose right now is to balance the body and energy around it.*

Allow no history or story or other factor to interrupt your process. You are surrounding yourself in light. The light is working for you on your behalf by creating vitality and balance.

Part B

- Once your body is relaxed, visualise breathing into a point shaped like a small star about 20 centimetres (8 inches) above your head.

- Now visualise a small star floating the same distance below your feet, along the centreline of your spine.

- With your being completely filled with light, simultaneously breathe into the star above your head and the star below, and into your feet.

- Now expand the stars as your energy field grows bigger and illuminates further. Expand the field as much as feels comfortable. Use your intuition! Do this for 3 to 5 minutes.

- Release the breath and focus on the feelings in your body for 3 minutes in silence to complete the process.

RELEASING STAGNATED ENERGY

Try this exercise anytime you feel weighed down.

- Sit quietly in meditation for 2 to 3 minutes, simply focusing on each inhale and exhale, and letting any thoughts drift away like clouds in the sky.

- Ask the Spirit to guide your hands.

- Set the intention to clear the energy of each chakra.

- Focusing on the root chakra, close your eyes, take both your hands and spin them over your crown chakra counter-clockwise 7 times and then cast the energy upwards for the Light or Source to absorb.

- Now do the same for the sacral chakra, spinning your hands 7 times around the head just above the crown chakra, counter clockwise, and releasing the energy upwards.

- Now move onto the solar plexus, then the heart, throat, third eye and crown.

- Finish by thanking the Spirit for clearing your energy.

- Meditate for 2 to 3 minutes more in silence.

Move your hands counter-clockwise to clear each chakra.

All of these exercises are simple but powerful. If you find yourself still feeling out of sorts or stagnant after adopting some of these new practices, try working with angelic healing (see pages 154–161). Or it may be time to find a trained and experienced energy practitioner in your area to assist you. Just don't give up.

The more often you consciously enter states of balance and peace, the more you will train your energy. I call this *vibrational entrainment*. It's like developing muscle memory as an athlete. You wouldn't run a marathon without training, just like you cannot expect to be a master of something that you've only just begun practising. Ultimately everyone has the power to self-heal, to open their minds, expand their energy and empower their beings.

DON'T UNDERESTIMATE THE
POWER OF THE HUMAN SPIRIT

2. UNLOCK YOUR POWER

The old divides between magic and science are blurring. Both ancient wisdom and modern technologies continue to offer us incredible amounts of useful information and insights. Today, there are multitudes of opportunities available for those of us seeking change and growth. New discoveries continue to flow from the disciplines of medicine, psychology and consciousness development. Culture by culture, awareness by awareness, we are developing our understanding and gaining fresh results with each approach. We are merging our ideologies daily.

Shamanic visions, experienced hundreds, even thousands of years ago, once helped develop systems for opening our minds. Today, recent studies of brain waves in meditative states have revealed direct correlations between healing, relaxation and neurology. Chinese medicine treatments such as acupuncture, herbal remedies, acupressure and bodywork

use a meridian system whereby energy moves along channels
for the regulation of the Life Force. Some healing systems
call upon angels, or guides, bringing messages from Spirit,
to participate in the treatments. Everywhere around us,
there is a blending of the seen and the unseen. Mystics and
physicists alike have their own methods of coming to the same
conclusion: that time is non-linear. Getting into a non-linear
mind space or a spacious mindset is the optimum condition for
the healer to perform a healing.

Yet how can all these systems have so many variations and
origins – and still have any resonance with each other?
How do plant medicines from the Amazon cultures and the
Native American cultures relieve long-term chronic disease?
Their nutritional properties? The spirit of the plant? Is it the
intention? Or all three?

ENERGY HEALING SYSTEMS

As we have seen, energy follows intention. We are all electromagnetic beings, processing thoughts and emotions, both individually and in groups – and who knows how many ways we affect each other daily with our energy? Frequency is a carrier of all sorts of information, and, as we cultivate our awareness by tapping into different sources of knowledge, we retune ourselves energetically and expand into a greater sense of who we are. We are still evolving and learning, and we need to continue to do so as part of our journey here on Earth.

Medicine is perfecting the process of scanning energy in the human body in more and more precise ways. Therapeutic approaches to healing the mind are using creative and adaptive resources to change our energy. Polarity therapy, EMDR and Brainspotting are just a couple of examples of systems that connect therapeutic healing with creative energetic approaches. Acupuncture is now an approach accepted by the mainstream to treat stress, illness and pain.

There are many pathways in the body that can be accessed to promote healing. On the following pages, you will find some examples of disciplines and treatments that deploy a mix of modern science, energy, spiritual practice, sound and light, consciousness and Life-Force energy to promote healing. You might find that some of these are very interesting to you and others may not be. Notice what draws you. See what looks appealing to you. Enjoy the options!

Colour Therapy

Also known as chromotherapy, one of the earliest known usages of colour therapy originated in ancient Egypt. The Egyptians built temples with stained-glass windows to allow the Sun's rays to filter through different coloured glass throughout the day. Then people lay down to receive, or 'bathe', in the various frequencies of light filtering through the windows at different times of day for their perceived healing properties.

Light has the ability to penetrate deeply into the physical body, energising the skin and blood cells. Specific colours can be used to balance the major energy centres of the body (see 'Your Primary Energy Centres – the Chakras', page 64), which can become stagnant as we experience life's difficulties. Artists and sages have known for centuries that colour influences our moods and emotional states; thus it also has an effect on our energy flow.

Colour, just like light, is a language of the inner spirit. However, there are nuances in each healing system, as a colour might have one effect on an energy centre (or chakra) and another in the form of light acting on the brain, for instance.

In energy healing, individual colours serve their own specific healing purpose:

RED: warmth, energy, strength, determination, passion, sexuality, assertiveness, stimulation, independence.

ORANGE: warmth, productivity, pleasure, cheerfulness, freedom, possibility, creativity.

YELLOW: positivity, vitality, exuberance, celebration, willpower, confidence, persuasion, happiness, stimulation.

GREEN: peace, balance, rest, healing, harmony, purification, love, abundance, health, nature, growth, fertility, family, inner peace.

BLUE: honesty, depth, cooling, communication, honour, calming, understanding, protection during sleep, dreamy, magical, rational, powerful, humility.

INDIGO: cooling, electric, astringent, purification, vision, stability, truth, higher perception, depth, power, mental acuity, psychic awareness.

VIOLET: transformation, stability, soothing anxiety and stress, divination, angels, royalty, spiritual power, wisdom, mystery, meditation, dignity, sensitivity, detoxification.

WHITE: perfection, Universal healing, purification, innocence, balance, awakening, consciousness, cleansing, enlightenment. (When all the different colours of light are combined, white light is created, and working with white light brings about feelings of completeness and oneness.)

MAGENTA: strengthens life purpose, stimulates heart, magnetism, sound, music, passion, creativity, self-realisation, focus, power.

PINK: femininity, softness, light, gentleness, compassion, kindness, youthfulness, love.

TURQUOISE: intuition, sensitivity, relaxation, good fortune, bright skin, originality, invention, freedom, depth, innovation, humanity.

SILVER: neutrality, calming, stillness, patience, cool, reservation.

BLACK: underworld, protection, binding, banishing, deep meditation, unconscious self, seriousness, mystery, completion of a cycle/death, silence, extremes: everything and nothing, self-trust. (In painting, when all the colours are combined they form black – just as they combine as white in light.)

Colour therapy is the reason why art can heal! Painting, fashion, interior design and feng shui can create balance and harmony through colour. Sometimes painting a child's room a different colour can relax the space. Doctors' offices are now designed using colour to be friendly to the eye and restful to the being.

Chromotherapy sunglasses, sometimes called colour therapy or chakra therapy glasses, are coloured lenses that offer the healing benefits of colour and can be worn at home or during healing therapy sessions.

Wear coats of many colours

Experiment with wearing different colours to add energy or specific frequencies to your day.

Sound Healing

Chanting, mantras, drumming, singing, binaural beats (sound frequencies where the right and left ears are listening to slightly different tones but perceive them as one) and playing instruments are all forms of the ancient practice of sound healing. Sound waves interact with everything and touch every part of our physical being. Tibetans and Sikhs use gongs. Aboriginals use didgeridoos. Shamanic cultures from all over the world use various kinds of flutes and drums.

Sound is formed by electromagnetic waves that interact with energy, water, matter and the eardrum to activate liquid crystals in the cells of the human body. Sound can even structure water molecules! Sound is vibration that touches every part of our being. We don't just hear it, we feel it. Certain frequencies can calm the mind and have a neurological effect, putting the brain from an alpha into a theta brainwave state – the state of mind achieved in meditation and deep relaxation.

Sound can create healing channels from several directions: the ears, the mind, the energy and the cells in the body. You might have heard of, or tried, sound bowls? Singing bowls, another name for sound healing bowls, have been used in Eastern traditions down the ages. Some are made of metal and used for meditation purposes. However, I personally work with crystal sound bowls to integrate both their sound healing properties and crystal technology for transmitting energy (see 'Crystals', pages 100–102): quartz crystal sound healing is an integral part of my practice. When a crystal sound bowl attuned to a healing frequency is played, the note that is activated corresponds to one of the seven major energy centres of the body (see pages 64–72), starting with the root chakra and the note middle C. Each note tunes and balances the associated energy centre, which in turn connects with a vital organ of the body.

Alchemy bowls are crystal sound healing bowls infused with additional minerals, gemstones or metals that aid a specific aspect of healing. For example, if a person is having physical heart problems and wants to incorporate an alternative therapy for home use, they might want to purchase an Alchemy bowl infused with rose quartz (which works on the heart chakra), in the musical note of F, which also addresses the heart centre.

Using a gong in meditation is also extremely powerful. According to yogic philosophy, the gong is the source of all sound and music. As a complete vibratory system, it puts the listener in a state of deep relaxation and peace, while stimulating the glandular system to function at higher levels, quieting the mind and releasing blockages and tension.

'Music is
the bridge
between worlds.'

EDGAR CAYCE, CLAIRVOYANT

Try downloading some sound healing online that incorporates pure crystal tones or check out a kundalini yoga class that incorporates a gong meditation at the end. You might find it interesting to try a group 'sound bath', which uses crystal or alchemy singing bowls. Enjoy the exploration!

Crystals

Crystals are as old as our 4.6 billion-year-old planet. They are sort of like the Earth's geological record keepers and today they are used to heal or adorn a body or a physical space. Crystals can be used on their own or in conjunction with other healing methods. There is a lot of science and spiritual understanding that goes into the complexity of therapeutic-grade quartz crystals for healing. One leader in this field, Dr Marcel Vogel, studied how the composition and geometric shape of precisely cut quartz can convert and amplify energy, to influence the human energy field.

At their core, crystals can be likened to frozen light. The word 'crystal' actually comes from the Greek *crystallos*, meaning 'frozen light'. A perfect molecular and energetic patterning is contained within the crystal's physical structure, which, when precisely cut, can be used as an energy device to balance, organise and smooth the human energy field – or even the vibrations in a space.

Crystals can also restructure your drinking water. The late Dr Masaru Emoto studied how human consciousness can affect the molecular structure of water, including through prayer and positive visualisation. Water and crystals can both be charged by using our breath and intention, imbuing these neutral materials with a form of consciousness. Quartz crystals can store information and amplify energy. They are used in mobile phones, watches, clocks and other modern technology because they oscillate at a precise frequency. Because crystals emit positive energy, using them in your meditations, wearing them or placing them around your home creates a balanced and nourishing environment.

Working with crystals at home is a great way to start sensing subtle energies and to experience the benefits of their healing properties. As suggested on pages 46–47, try placing an amethyst in your left hand while doing meditative breathing exercises and see if you can sense the subtle energy contributing to your state of peace. As we saw in Part One of this book, amethyst helps you connect to spiritual planes, while also sharpening the mind, protecting your field and grounding your energy.

If you are having trouble fully engaging at work, try placing pyrite, or 'fool's gold' on your desk. Pyrite will help you get the job done while staying determined and focused. (For more information on which gemstones and crystals assist the energy of each chakra, see pages 64–72.)

Magnetic Therapy

Since the discovery of the rock mineral magnetite, magnetic therapy has been used to correct imbalances in the Life-Force energy also known as qi (chi) and prana, as described in Chinese and Indian healing practices. Today, a person can lay on a mat embedded with small magnets that are strategically placed at certain meridian points, or energy centres, to help promote physical balance.

The benefits are physical as well as energetic, such as, for example, sending more oxygen to cell tissues, reducing swelling and pain and helping the body to detox. Magnets can aid new cell growth, as well as decrease inflammation, by activating cellular metabolism. They can also improve lymphatic circulation.

To benefit from magnetic therapy, it's best to work with a health professional who incorporates this modality into their practice. It may help promote sound sleep and reduce stress.

Reiki

Reiki is a Japanese form of energy healing that uses energy from the hands of the practitioner on or near the body of the recipient. The word 'Reiki' comes from the Japanese *Rei*, meaning

'God's wisdom' or 'Higher Power' and *Ki*, meaning 'Life-Force energy'. Dr Mikao Usui is credited with bringing the method out into the world in the 1920s.

Though the idea of channelling Life-Force energy is not new, the practice of doing it in a certain sequence as taught by Dr Usui is known specifically as Reiki. The practitioner is trained to generate and transmit Life-Force energy to those receiving the therapy. It is often deeply relaxing, is thought to help reduce pain and add energy to the healing process, and can also be used for distance healing. Reiki has influenced many other forms of hands-on energy healing and is a popular, non-evasive technique now found throughout the world.

Reiki can be incorporated into massage, other energy healing systems and these days even in facials! Through training and initiation, you can learn to perform Reiki on yourself or others. The first step would be to find the right practitioner for you. Then, if you are keen on the healing benefits of the practice, find an experienced Reiki master as your teacher.

Finding the Right Practitioner for You

The results achieved by energy healing techniques can vary from practitioner to practitioner, with some practitioners earning a reputation for significant healing outcomes while other practitioners achieve less obvious results. Some practitioners seem to achieve results when treating a specific kind of ailment, while others, even when using the same techniques, might not obtain comparable results for that issue.

With purely energetic healing practices, the integration of energies between the practitioner and client is key. Because using purely energetic healing systems relies on the practitioner's energy and is not about any external tools or technology, the resulting success is largely dependent on the healer's inner balance, vibration and experience level.

Polarity Therapy

Polarity therapy is an integrated healing system that was developed by Dr Rudolph Stone in the 1940s. It has elements of bodywork, awareness development, diet and hands-on energy work. Dr Stone, himself a multi-disciplinary doctor, studied Ayurvedic medicine in India as well as chiropractic, osteopathy and Eastern medicine.

Polarity therapy uses the electromagnetic field of the body to balance or alter positive and negative charges in order to optimise the flow of energy for better health. Its focus is on subtle energy alignment to help promote mental, emotional and physical wellbeing, and it is a gentle style of healing that is not physically demanding – the sessions can be very, very relaxing. Polarity therapy is now available worldwide, with thousands of practitioners. Emotional Freedom Technique or EFT (sometimes described as 'psychological acupressure' – a technique of tapping energy centres to create balance, thereby diminishing physical or emotional pain), sound healing (see page 97) or even supplements such as spirulina may also help alleviate polarity issues.

EMDR and Brainspotting

EMDR, or Eye Movement Desensitisation and Reprocessing, was first developed by Francine Shapiro in the 1980s, and can be very helpful in dealing with traumas and PTSD. It is a procedure- and protocol-driven therapy in which bilateral eye movements are coordinated with questions guided by the therapist. This stimulates the brain's awareness to locate a trauma within the brain's own network.

EMDR targets pain, anxiety or trauma, and expedites a release of these. It targets memories and has also been known to reduce the total therapy time. Some people also use it for performance anxiety too. It uses the limbic system and accesses channels that do not require the same kind of reasoning on the part of the client that might be expected from other kinds of behavioural or cognitive therapies. You don't need to understand it for it to succeed, for example, but simply to do the process, which mobilises interactions in the left and right sides of the brain.

Dr David Grand was trained in EMDR and developed his Brainspotting method in 2003, when working with survivors of trauma in his therapy practice, by observing and using eye positions to determine the locations of and access unprocessed trauma in the subcortical brain.

Brainspotting (BSP) can similarly be used to treat PTSD and negative emotions such as fear and anxiety, as well as to optimise performance (it is often used by elite athletes). It is a relational, brain–body, mindfulness-based therapy, which releases frozen energy trapped in the body by providing a way for the brain to access and then process the trauma. This is not a process you can do by yourself, as it needs to be facilitated by a professional. Over 13,000 therapists have been trained internationally in this practice, most often psychologists, psychiatrists, clinical social workers and other healthcare professionals.

Shamanism

From the dawn of humankind, peoples from around the globe had no choice but to work with the natural world for their very survival. The belief in animism, the concept that everything is conscious and alive, was a widely held mindset that assisted early indigenous people to connect to the world around them. Animism itself holds that the Universe is comprised of spiritual energies. Most ancient traditions uphold animist beliefs and humans evolved believing in the existence of the Life Force and in an interconnected world of nature and Spirit.

Shamans are usually dynamic leaders who guide their tribes and live in very close relationship with the land as well as the realms beyond. Shamans are naturally interested in cultivating power, so as the eternal students of life, they study and learn, and teach and lead. They are fearless, brave, courageous and deep. They are often artists, healers, doctors, warriors, hunters, sages, political figures, weather men and women, herbalists and masters of ceremonies. But more importantly, they are *inner warriors*. They walk the edge of the human condition and confront what most of us fear to face. Shamans spend their lives working to heal their own personal obstacles with that fearless nature of the inner warrior and are thus able to guide others along the path to understanding.

The shamanistic heart sees everything as energy. Whatever shines the brightest has the most power, despite its physical form: shamanism understands the difference between appearances and truth. Shamans were the first to act as emotional counsellors and to offer support systems, understanding the need for emotional energy to be processed and channelled in the most impactful way. In fact, modern counselling practices may have some shamanistic roots, as many infer that both Jung and Freud studied the subject to some extent.

Two common energy healing practices in many shamanistic traditions are spirit release and soul retrieval. Shamans believe that souls can get lost or stuck in the dimensions between life and death when crossing over to the other side at the end of life. This might occur for many reasons, so helping souls ascend at the time of death is a well-established part of shamanic practice. From the shamanic perspective, if a soul is in limbo it could become attached to a living person's energy field in an attempt to seek light. In this instance, a shaman would create an energetic portal around the living person and call on spiritual guides to assist in releasing the foreign entity into the light, while recalibrating the energy field of the person affected by the attachment.

Shamanism also believes that when a human experiences trauma that is too difficult for them to handle, parts of that person's energy field or consciousness can fragment outwards from the physical body into the Universe as a defense mechanism, causing aspects of their energy to be temporarily scattered. Soul fragmentation can leave you feeling mentally all over the place, not fully present, or disconnected from the physical body or life. This is sort of like the energetic parallel to disassociate behaviours in Western psychology. Shamans can perform a ceremony to call back all the spiritual energies of the person to be fully grounded in the physical body. This is called soul retrieval and has been practised for thousands of years in different ways by cultures all over the world.

The shamanic path is an Earth- and spirit-based lifestyle and philosophy, whose countless lineages go back over thousands of years, with many individual traditions that vary from tribe to tribe. There is no structured, 'one size fits all' shamanic system, although there are some common energetic practices found across cultures.

However, these practices are not something you can do at home – you will need to find an experienced practitioner. But the good news is that you don't have to be a shaman to live a life in accordance with shamanic principles!

So, what does that mean? It means being brave. It means being a proactive participant in your life experience. It means challenging yourself. This is not a path for the lazy or those who want to stay in their comfort zone. The shamanic path embodies a whole, sound and complete way of being that goes back at least 40,000 years and is the basis for spiritual understanding and human development on all continents.

SHAMANISM AND MOTHER EARTH

Mother Earth has her own electromagnetic field and the energies stemming from her many lifeforms offer various kinds of 'medicine' or healing properties; for example, the Life Force of the oceans and herbal remedies. Shamanic cultures honoured the Earth for all she gave to her children. The prevalent philosophy was a sacred, symbiotic relationship between man and the wild. Because of this fundamental connection, people made honouring the Earth a part of everyday life.

Earth's energy makes us feel at home in our human bodies because our field naturally expands in nature's presence. Living out of harmony with this power source means cutting off a supply of vitality. People often feel healthier and more peaceful farther away from the hustle and bustle of big cities for a reason.

Doing what you can to honour nature, the plants and animals, and connecting with wild places as often as you can, sends the energy of reverence and respect to shamanic cultures of the past and present as keepers of the Earth.

Earth Yourself

If you don't have a lot of time, *earthing* is the practice of putting your bare feet on natural ground and deeply breathing while intentionally connecting with Mother Earth's electromagnetic field. You could even try meditating with your feet in mud to help ground yourself.

By honouring the Earth, drumming, chanting, listening to nature, praying, meditating, facing your light and your shadow, being fearless, seeing the lessons in everything around you, slowing down, becoming your own chief, artist, healer, warrior, storyteller and by working with Spirit – you too can embody the heart of the shaman.

CACAO CEREMONY

According to Mayan and Aztec mythology, cacao was used not only as a source of food but in spiritual ceremonies to represent the Life Force. It was nourishment for their gods and a sacred offering, connecting the spiritual realms and the Earth. The Maya consumed cacao as a frothy, bitter beverage that was served hot.

To work on your connection to sacred Earth elements, hold a personal cacao ceremony at an auspicious time, like a full or new Moon, your birthday or to open or close a life chapter. Shamanism is without dogma, and it is creative!

Check out this 2000-year-old recipe, optimised for modern times:

• Purchase high-quality ceremonial cacao or cacao paste.

• Chop up approximately 3 tablespoons cacao and put it in a blender with ¾–1 cup hot water.

• Add spices or sacred edible ingredients like organic dried rose petals, chilli peppers or lavender to taste.

• As you chop, add and mix the ingredients, keep a specific intention in mind. Remember, energy follows intention and you want your vibration and intention to serve as an ingredient in this ceremonial beverage.

- Add any healthy sweeteners such as agave, honey, dates and flower nectars or superfood supplements like maca or chaga mushroom if you wish. (Traditionally no sweetener is used but this is YOUR ceremony. Do it how you want to.)

- The resulting drink should be frothy, thick and creamy.

- Light some candles, set out some crystals or burn white ceremonial sage to set the tone in your chosen quiet place.

- Write down your intention on a piece of paper.

- As you sip your drink, imagine drinking in your intention and thanking the Universe for supporting the manifestation.

- When finished, burn the paper in a burning bowl.

- Sit quietly for 2 to 3 minutes in meditation.

- Thank the Mayan lineage for discovering and activating this type of ritual so that we can use it in our modern lives.

NOTES: *Cacao paste is made from cacao beans that are fermented, lightly roasted or sun dried, and then ground. It becomes solid at room temperature and there is only one ingredient in it. Ceremonial cacao uses only native cacao strains from South America. It is considered a superfood.*

CHARGING YOUR POWER CENTRE

Sometimes we need a recharge! The body and its energy need
to be revitalised. We might not have a lot of time to spare,
but we need to be fresh and sharp. This is when we can do a
power centre meditation that connects with the Life Force around
us in nature.

- Close your eyes in a comfortable sitting position in nature,
  preferably next to a tree.

- Take a deep inhale into your solar plexus (see page 68
  for the chakra position), hold it for about 2 seconds, then
  release the breath.

- Become aware of how the energy coming in with your
  inhales balances with the energy leaving with your exhales.
  Meditate on this balance and integration in your solar plexus
  – your power centre.

- Breathe in through your nose and out through your mouth.
  The breath should be full but should not make you dizzy or
  light-headed.

- Repeat this 12 times.

- Feel your lungs expand. Feel your ribs move.

- Feel this energy centre expand into a brilliant, shining sun
  the size of a bowling ball. Through the power of your
  intention and imagination, make this sun grow bigger
  and bigger, until the light emanates from you and you are
  encased in a sphere of your own power.

- Visualise a Tree of Wisdom, with deep roots and protective
  branches sheltering you inside this power sphere.

- Mentally ask this Tree to guide you in making wise choices
  that support your personal power.

- Sit with this Tree and receive healing.

- When completed, remain silent for 2 to 3 minutes.

THE MAORI TRADITION

Atarangi Muru is an elder in the Maori lineage – a lineage
to which I feel blessed to have a connection through my
loved ones. She describes how the teaching of various arts –
including carving, *pounamu* (greenstone treasures), gardening,
the Maramataka (their Moon calendar), child bearing, child
rearing, healing, bush herbs and medicines, genealogy,
tribal stories and the like – were all taught orally to younger
generations by the elders.

The elders would, for instance, nurture a mother-to-be as she
carried her child, watching to see what indications Mother Earth
gave of the child's gifts. Children born feet first are revered
in Maori tradition for their physical abilities, and a child born
with a high instep is associated with the gift of a photographic
memory, and would thus be taught the *whakaapa* (genealogy) –
the Maori stories of the land, the sea and the sky.

Whatever the child's predicted talents, an elder would sing a
birth song for the child and, in it, speak to the child's courage,
strength, big heartedness and patience. They would weave a
pathway of energy and love for this child to take them from pre-
birth to birth, childhood, teenage years, adulthood and finally
to eldership. A connection to God, the Earth, water, rain, wind,

currents of the tide and the sea were all included in the birth song if this child came from a coastal area. If the child was from further inland, they would talk of the trees, the plants, gardening and the gathering of food. Then, at the end of life, the grown person's death song would be sung, which would speak of their achievements both inside and outside the tribe. When an individual is raised like this, the teachings are said to be 'bone deep', repeated throughout his or her life. In this way, the Maori stay in a strong soul alignment with their culture and traditions.

Bodywork

Bodywork is an umbrella term for a range of physical methods for bringing healing benefits and relaxation to the body, including popular practices such as the Alexander technique and shiatsu. Some methods combine the physical and the energetic. Some directly address sports issues or clinical injuries, while other, older forms integrate Life-Force energies, shamanic practices or spiritual disciplines to clear channels in the physical body and promote healing through cleansing those channels and releasing blockages. By working at a deep-tissue level with the muscles, the skeleton and the structure of the body, it is possible to achieve emotional, mental and physiological realignments through bodywork.

Because all is connected, mental, physical, or emotional imbalances can be stored in the physical body at various levels. You could uncover and release a suppressed emotional wound from working through physical pain, for instance; or conversely be fully aware of an emotional wound yet find bodywork an impactful method of release. Bodywork is a profound form of healing, especially if you find a practitioner who is skilled in both the structural aspects of the human body and also the more psychological, intuitive and energetic worlds.

Emotion is a form of energy; in fact, it is actually energy in motion. Emotions can be likened to physiological responses to thought processes in the conscious or subconscious mind. When we do not cope in healthy ways with trauma, the emotions associated with the hurt will remain active in the mind, energy and body until healed, released and balanced. If this occurs, your body will tell you when something is off. It is the vehicle for your spirit and has its own intelligence. It will talk to you and tell you what it needs, if you are willing to listen.

Bodywork systems often assist the nervous and parasympathetic nervous systems in helping you to relax. They can also stimulate the lymphatic system, which helps with detoxification. They can bring your spine or hips into alignment, or help release tension in the muscles. There are various systems for mapping ailments and dysfunctions and for achieving structural alignment within bodywork. Some of those systems, like orthopaedics, are centred around skeletal alignment; some of them, like osteopathy, include soft tissue and muscular-skeletal manipulation; and some forms use pressure and movement to release energy.

Take acupressure and tui na, for example. Acupressure uses physical hand movements to place pressure on certain energy points, thereby activating the body's self-healing mechanism. Tui na is a Chinese form of bodywork that works with the same energy centres or channels as the practice of Traditional Chinese Medicine for moving energy in the physical body.

Craniosacral therapy is another non-invasive, hands-on healing practice for treating physical pain, trauma, abstract tension (where the source is tough to pinpoint) and discomfort in the body. It's a meditative approach that addresses a huge range of physical, psychological, psychosomatic and psycho-spiritual ailments. It takes into consideration the energetic and physical processes of embryology and birth as formative patterns in our systems.

Myofascial release is yet another form of bodywork that focuses on pain or stored trauma in the connective tissue.

Keep a Clear Head

Anything you can do by yourself that addresses the physical health of your body will support energetic alignment. Do your own research on various kinds of bodywork and massage practices, and see what resonates with you.

In the meantime, try massaging the acupressure points shown in the diagram below the next time you have a headache.

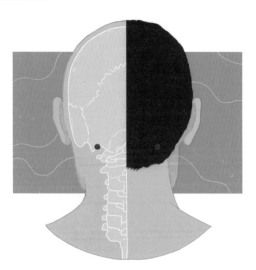

Traditional Chinese medicine (TCM)

Chinese medicine has been practised for over 3,500 years. During this time many different healing methods and strands were developed, influenced by various shamanic styles, incantation and divination work, as well as Buddhist and Taoist theory.

TCM, as it is known today, was reorganised and reinstated by Chairman Mao in the 1950s. When Western medicine became too costly to import, Mao rounded up the most famous healers and practitioners from around China to devise a system that drew together the various indigenous methods for rebalancing the body, with a focus on the health of the major organs.

The ancient Taoist concepts of yin and yang also feature in TCM. These can be thought of as two complementary, interconnected and interdependent forces, with the yin relating to the negative, passive and female principles in nature, whereas the yang is the positive, active and male principle.

Today, acupuncture, herbal formulas, tui na, moxibustion and qi gong are all part of the Traditional Chinese Medicine system. Acupuncture is one of my own go-to therapies when I am feeling depleted and need to rejuvenate my sense of vitality.

ACUPUNCTURE

An acupuncturist will concentrate on activating points of energy that stimulate the flow of qi (chi) in meridians, or lines of energy, throughout the physical body, which relate to a specific set of symptoms or health concerns. Energy centres are opened and stimulated by the subtle puncturing of the skin with extremely fine needles that you can barely feel. The practitioner gets more qi flowing to the chosen centres through this stimulation as a way to restore balance. It is also very common for a practitioner to suggest a set of herbs to take alongside regular treatments to facilitate the healing process.

SCHISANDRA

Schisandra was described in China's first herbal dictionary, in the first century BC, as being a superior herb that can be used daily to promote longevity and wellbeing – a fact that remains true today. Schisandra tincture can be sourced through your local Chinese Medicine practitioner or obtained online.

Schisandra is so powerful partly to due to the fact that it features all five of the main types of taste at once, each with its own medicinal application:

SWEET: restores energy and the immune system.

SALTY: provides minerals and nourishes the blood.

SOUR: detoxes and promotes digestion.

BITTER: stimulates digestion, treats inflammation and detoxes.

PUNGENT: strengthens organs, stimulates blood circulation and is especially beneficial to the lungs and colon.

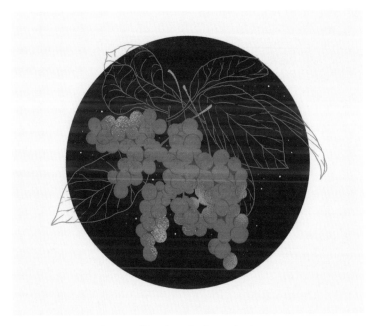

Clusters of bright red schisandra berries.

- **LIVER DETOX (LIVER QI STAGNATION)**: one of schisandra's greatest attributes is its ability to cleanse the liver because of its strong antioxidant properties. It assists the detoxification process by helping to bind waste and toxins and eliminate them from the body, and stimulates the growth of new liver cells. It also helps to shield the liver from those toxins to which it is exposed either environmentally or through food.

- **STRESS (LIVER AND ADRENAL YIN DEFICIENCIES)**: schisandra is quite effective as an adaptogen. Because this herb works for liver harmony, it addresses the adrenals by responding to excess stress through modulating endocrine and immune functions. Schisandra combats symptoms of a poor metabolism such as fatigue, lack of endurance, frequent infections and blood sugar swings, as well as the effects of stress and over-work, by balancing the adrenal cortex and liver.

- **LUNG AND KIDNEY (YANG DEFICIENCIES)**: schisandra harmonises lung and kidney yang deficiencies by restoring and oxygenating the lungs. The herb helps treat the following symptoms: chronic coughing, wheezing, shortness of breath, altitude sickness and respiratory infections. This herb heals and oxygenates the lungs.

- **KIDNEY (QI DEFICIENCIES):** schisandra balances kidney fluids and overall strengthens the kidney qi. Some examples of imbalances may include night sweats and frequent urination.

- **COLD INTESTINES (SPLEEN AND KIDNEY YANG DEFICIENCIES):** the herb has a positive effect on symptoms such as chronic diarrhoea, bloating and stomach discomfort by promoting circulation in the digestive tract. These actions also boost the immune system.

- **HEART HEALTH:** schisandra helps to lower blood pressure and improve heart health by improving blood flow, leading to healthier blood vessels.

- **SKIN HEALTH (YIN DEFICIENCY WITH DRYNESS):** schisandra has always been popular in China, especially among the wealthy, for promoting beautiful skin and providing protection from Sun and wind damage. In a painting from ancient times, Magu, the goddess of beauty and eternal youth, is pictured serving a tray of schisandra, reishi (the herb of immortality) and a 'peach of longevity' to her immortal friends. The astringent nature of schisandra helps the skin to hold moisture to keep it plump and supple. Schisandra also helps to improve problems like eczema and hives because of its power to heal the liver.

Schisandra energises, strengthens, protects and nourishes all the organs and meridians of the body. It balances hormones, improves mental and cognitive function, promotes beautiful skin and is an anti-ageing herb. Schisandra is believed to benefit all functions of the body, with its greatest influence being on kidney, lung and liver function.

A Word of Caution

Make sure you consult your primary medical practitioner when using herbs as, although they are natural products, they are powerful and can have strong effects.

Breathwork

Using breath and intention for the purposes of healing is a practice that is thousands of years old and which has evolved in many different ways. However, a new technique has been birthed in healing circles in NYC and LA. Breathwork, as the term is known today, is an active meditation that focuses on breath combined with energy to clear and cleanse the body and its energy of emotional stagnation.

From an energetic and vibrational medicine perspective, I find breathwork incredibly powerful and work with many students and teachers from that community because it really complements and aligns with my own practice. Energy stagnation can easily be traced back to emotional wounds – both the core wound, as well as consequent behaviours and mental constructs that stem from that wound.

Most people, whether consciously or not, have an aversion to healing old emotional wounds. Cultivating emotional health can be messy and feel uncomfortable. Yet the emotional body holds powerful energy, and true mastery does not come from intellectual understanding, but from emotional understanding. You have to feel a truth in your emotions, body and energy to take full advantage of that wisdom. While you may understand mentally and intellectually that joy can arise from powerfully loving yourself, you won't master that understanding until you really feel it in your bones as the truth of who you are. Emotions such as shame, guilt, fear, loneliness, isolation and unworthiness can limit your ability to embrace big love. Breathwork is a technique that may penetrate through those layers to help you experience freedom.

Breathwork teaches you to look at your emotions without judgement and with complete compassion for yourself and others. It brings clarity, self-acceptance, intimacy and a sense of community. With time, practice and patience, long-lasting energetic balance occurs. Source energy travels on the breath. This is an ancient knowing.

Breathwork teachers, groups and retreats offer a wonderful way to bring Light to each and every cell in your body, and release the pain that is holding you back. Erin Telford is the friend and healer who introduced me to this work. She is a Breathwork facilitator, acupuncturist, Reiki Master, herbalist and a teacher of David Elliott's Level One Breathwork Healer Training. Her work guides people to look within, open their hearts and heal their relationship with themselves. Erin and David are incredible trailblazers for this kind of work. I encourage you to do your own research to see what practitioners or resources may be available in your area.

Cosmic Energies

If I asked you and other readers if the waning and waxing of the Moon affected you, I would probably get a massive YES.

In this context, we are talking about how cosmic energies such as vibrations from the Sun, moon, planetary systems, constellations and space might be affecting the energy

'The nitrogen in our DNA, the calcium in our teeth, the iron in our blood, the carbon in our apple pies were made in the interiors of collapsing stars. We are made of star stuff.'

CARL SAGAN, COSMOLOGIST

on Earth. We can look at this from an astrological, Vedic, shamanic or Eastern perspective – and I encourage you to explore all of them.

The Sun is traditionally a representation of masculine energy, or dynamic energy. It is about fire, Life Force, vitality, positivity, energy, dynamic right action, exuberance, confidence, health, boldness, creativity and play. It is yang energy. The Moon is a representation of feminine energy or magnetic energy. This aspect is about water, mystery, silence, creating from stillness, addressing your inner worlds, dreams, emotions and bringing forth life from the void. This is yin energy. (When I talk about masculine or feminine energies, please note this actually has nothing to do with gender. All humans have both masculine and feminine energies within them internally that require balancing and integration.) Masculine refers to yang energy, or dynamic energy. Feminine energy refers to yin, or magnetic energy.

Working with the Moon when full, new, waxing or waning can help amplify the energy of a specific intention, while connecting us to the natural rhythms of the Earth. Life is either in a state of expansion or contraction, and the stages of the Moon parallel this concept.

Rituals give our energy and thoughts actionable form as containers to point and channel our consciousness in the right direction. The regular practice of ritual – for example, a full Moon ritual (see page 136) – can help us tune in to the interconnected natural system around us, instead of reacting against it.

FULL MOON RITUAL FOR CALLING IN ABUNDANCE

You will need: organic rose petals, a bowl filled with water, a £5 note/$10 bill, a metal burning bowl, a notepad and pen, 1 white candle, 1 green candle, 1 pink candle, 1 violet candle, 1 citrine crystal, 1 aventurine crystal, 1 rose quartz crystal, 1 malachite crystal.

- For 3 days prior to the full Moon, pick organic rose petals from the flower and mentally affirm: *I am love. I am abundant. I am wealth.*

- Place the rose petals in the bowl with water.

- Place your pound note or dollar bill in the rose petal water to cleanse it. (This is intended to symbolically cleanse your subconscious mind of any fears, judgements, anxieties or false stories you have around money.)

- Leave the pound note or dollar bill out to dry on a sacred altar where you meditate, or in a safe place outside under the building moonlight.

- Repeat this process with the same note or bill for the next 2 nights.

- On the night of the full Moon, write down this affirmation on your piece of paper:

  My True Self swims in the current of Spirit's infinite abundance. I am my True Self. Great currents of wealth circulate through all areas of my life easily and effortlessly. I am blessed by the abundance in my life. I give as I receive. And I receive in the name of love, joy and for the purposes of spreading light to others.

  Support in the form of wealth helps me live in expanded states of consciousness and helps me to care for myself, my family, my friends and community. Support in the form of wealth helps me to create from a place of inspiration, and love from a place of security.

  I am a child of the light. I am the love of that light. And because I AM, I am prosperous in all ways, and in all directions of time and space.

  Amen.

- Take the piece of paper and put it in the burning bowl.

- Place the burning bowl down and position the 4 candles securely around it.

- Place the cleansed dollar bill underneath the burning bowl.

- Put all the crystals in your hands and bless them with your intention mentally.

- Place a crystal next to each of the 4 candles.

- Light the candles.

- Read your abundance affirmation out loud, then burn it in the metal bowl.

- Meditate for 7 minutes on the idea that you already have everything you need in this moment present to the world around you and the world within you.

- The next day, take your pound note or dollar bill and deposit it in your bank account.

I did this practice for weeks when I worked with the Moon before starting my healing business. Of course, it took various other forms of effort to get here – but hey, look who's writing a book now? I guess I did something right!

Ritual is where divinity meets the material.

Sun-healing Practice

When you have an illness, or feel anxious, confused or depressed, go outside and put the palms of your hands up to the Sun while doing intentional deep breathing for a few minutes. It is powerfully rejuvenating. The Life Force and light from the Sun's rays move into the body, consciousness, mind and energy fields, revitalising the spirit.

For men and women who have been through any kind of sexual traumas, finding a safe, private spot where you can lie down and open your legs to take in the sun's light can bring healing and safety to sacred parts of the body that have been harmed. Even spending 7 to 11 minutes meditating on your willingness to heal, while open to the sun, can have profound benefits.

MAGIC IS SCIENCE
WE DON'T UNDERSTAND YET

Astrological Guidance

Each sign of the zodiac is associated with a particular planet, constellation and a set of archetypal energies. In natal and predictive astrology, when the Sun, Moon or a planet such as Jupiter, Mars or Venus falls into alignment with a particular constellation, the converging energies are believed to convey a theme or tone relating to an individual person's phase of life. We can use this information to make sense of our experiences.

Some people view astrology as the oldest system to offer a psychological map with which to chart your personality in depth, as well as uncover its nuances. It's like a personality test you don't have to take. If you book a session with an experienced and intuitive astrologer, all you will need to provide is your birth date, location and time. Looking at your natal chart and how the stars and planets were aligned at the time of your birth can help you to understand yourself on a deeper level. Equipped with this information, you can make more informed decisions.

I know people who consult astrologers before making business investments, when meeting a new partner or when moving through big transitions. An awareness of astrological aspects and influences can help you discern which dominant cosmic energies would be most advantageous to harness at a given point in time.

The Age of Aquarius

Approximately every 2,150 years, a new astrological age begins that is named according to which constellation is visible behind the vernal equinox sunrise. The Age of Aquarius relates to our current astrological era, the energy of these times and how humanity's collective energy is being activated by the cyclical planetary patterns at play. According to Sikh masters, we entered the Age of Aquarius officially as of 11 November 2011. However, we have been on the cusp of this global, energetic shift since 1991. (I've personally been hearing about this shift in songs and from healers, writers and spiritual teachers, and in my own personal meditations since my teenage years. When I attended Kundalini Yoga Teacher Training at Golden Bridge NYC in the early 2000s, we got into it a bit more deeply.) There are many other schools of thought relating to when the astrological Aquarian age officially started and what is happening because of that shift, so my explanation here will be broad but brief.

An astronomer will affirm that Earth rotates on an axis that is not perfectly stable. A little circular, pulsating quiver affects the axis line in a cycle lasting about 24,000 years, which results in the precession of the equinoxes. In astrology, this period has been divided into 12 'months' of approximately 2,160 years each, which are in turn associated with the 12 astrological signs. As we have seen, each astrological sign has its own character, attributes and overarching archetypal theme. Each of the 12-part 'months' or 'ages' are named for the constellation or astrological sign towards which the axis moves, with the centre of the Earth vibrating towards a different sign roughly every 2000 years or so. For example, approximately 2160 BCE to 0 CE marked the Age of Aries; whereas from 0 CE until very recently, we've been in the Age of Pisces, which was dominated by machines, dogma and hierarchies.

At the dawn of the Age of Aquarius, we can expect greater awareness, open communication, sharing, transparency and information. Rapid technological advancements and globalisation mean we are constantly inundated with information and moving pieces, which really affect our nervous systems, as I discussed in the introduction. It can feel totally overwhelming! But all we need to do is upgrade our self-care practices to help us remain centred and open during this transition in human history. When you learn to hold space for yourself, you can do so for others too.

Yoga

Yoga has roots dating back at least 40,000 years, paralleling the timeline of shamanistic tradition, oddly enough. This was when the first real, systemised yogic practices were openly taught and integrated in communities.

Yogi Bhajan once said, 'I will tell you about yoga in very simple terms: The human mind is potentially Infinite and Creative. But in practical reality it is limited. So a technical know-how is required through which one can expand their mind to bring about the equilibrium that enables them to control their physical structure and experience their Infinite Selves.'

Yoga comes from the Sanskrit word meaning 'union'. The practice of yoga brings the individual consciousness together with infinite consciousness. A yogi or yogini is one who has merged with Spirit fully, totally and completely. One who studies yoga gains an understanding of what can be accomplished through combining asana (poses), meditation, dharma (a teaching, pillar or understanding of reality), mantra, diet, pranayama (breathing practices), lifestyle and discipline.

I've noticed that the study and practice of yoga provides a wonderful catalyst and opening point for people who want

to dive deeper into the world of healing. If nothing else, committing to yoga and meditation several times a week will improve your quality of life. Anytime we combine movement, breath, intention and stillness for the purposes of healing, we move closer into the Light. Yoga is an easily accessible and powerful way to do just that.

I enjoy Kundalini yoga as a full energetic system, although I've been taking all kinds of yoga classes since I was 14 years old and continue to incorporate them into my life. Because it is such an ancient practice and a large industry, with 22 variants and continued evolutions of yoga being created even today, you really have to try different forms and study with different yoga teachers to discover what works for you.

All yoga works to raise our Kundalini energy, which is how we raise our consciousness. But what is Kundalini? It is your full creative potential and power. It is the essence of consciousness. Kundalini energy lies coiled up at the base of the spine until we begin to activate it. This is why I was drawn to Kundalini yoga as a student, as it is the mother of all yogas. It incorporates sound, mantra, meditation and energy-balancing practices with asana as a complete science and system.

As a complement to Kundalini yoga, I enjoy intelligent, alignment-centred Vinyasa classes that offer depth and meditation. Others might enjoy a Hatha practice for mastering the polarities or an Ashtanga practice, which is the discipline of the 8 limbs as described by the Indian sage Patanjali, and follows a specific set of postures.

A faster-paced Vinyasa flow might be more aligned with those of you wanting to enjoy its relaxing and calming benefits combined with an intensive physical workout. Yin or restorative classes work at a slower pace and focus on your inner, silent worlds. If recovering from loss, injury or chronic stress, this might be a good place to start. Practising yoga in a heated room assists the detoxification process of the physical body.

Karma and Ancestral Energy Clearing

Karma is the law of cause and effect associated with our mental, moral and physical actions. According to the principles of karma, every action creates a reaction. Every cause has an effect. We can intentionally create a peaceful life by choosing to act with integrity, with Light and with loving intention. Reacting to a situation only creates further cause-and-effect manifestations.

When you recognise that the effect has no creation point, you begin to see that harping on about, or overreacting to an undesirable condition is a fool's errand. You can change what is to come through curating the conditions required to create balance. What is happening now is an effect of what was. And we cannot change the past or what is. But we can liberate ourselves by living beyond cause and effect. This is living with intention. This is living our dharma – the path of love and compassion.

Releasing karma for healing is a Westernisation of the original concept, and is about changing our life patterns by mastering a lesson associated with our past actions and behaviours. Once we learn the lesson, the pattern ceases to exist and the Universe no longer delivers the same 'spiritual curriculum'. We can look at the patterns in our life and search deeply within ourselves to find the root causes of their continued effects. More often than not, we are the ones standing in the way of our full power. With awareness, we can alter those patterns.

Not only can we accumulate karmic effects ourselves and accidentally strengthen the energetic patterns therein due to our ignorance or lack of intention to resolve them, but we can inherit karmic burdens from our family trees. Once we have an awareness of this, we can start to clear the past patterns, thereby healing the present and opening the way for future generations.

Our genetic and familial patterns can likewise be passed down from generation to generation. For example, if a great-great-grandmother had a lot of trauma around relationship and birth, she would very likely be protective and guarded with her daughter, without ever explaining the cause and effect of her fears, dilemmas or traumas around birth and sexuality. That daughter, not knowing the cause, would very likely pass down some of these guarded, hyper-vigilant behaviours to her own daughter. Four generations later, women in the same family tree could still be dealing with variations of these same issues with no knowledge whatsoever of their origins.

If you think you may be carrying the weight of past-generational suffering, try repeating the profound invocation on page 152 after a meditation.

GENERATIONAL CLEANSING PRAYER

We bless all beings in all time, all space and in all realms.

May all beings bless us.

I surround myself with love.

I fill the space around me and within me with the Divine.

I ask to be open to the wisdom of my deeper knowing.

I hereby release the darkness of despair, doubt, fear as well as the distortions of the mind and all energies and forces that create dysfunction, negativity and harm.

Begin with your parents:

- **BLESSING:** Bless my parents: may they bless and forgive each other, themselves, their parents and their children, and all generations to come. May they be open to receive this healing.

- **AFFLICTIONS – FIRST LAYER:** May the lineage bless those that have hurt them, done harm and damaged them. May they now release all the afflictions that have been created in the family. May they be given the consciousness to forgive completely and in turn be forgiven completely for those whom they have been harmful towards, in all directions of time and space.

- **FEAR – SECOND LAYER:** Bless them with light and release them from fear and the negative patterns perpetuated by fear – mentally, physically, emotionally, sexually, financially, psychologically, spiritually and in all directions of time and space.

- **GRATITUDE – THIRD LAYER:** We give thanks to all aspects of Spirit that have assisted us; known and unknown; named and unnamed; seen and unseen; that serve the highest good. We asked for the capacity to live in joy and hold gratitude for that which we have received and to share that feeling with others.

- **COMMANDMENT – FOURTH LAYER:** Light replaces burden. The chain is broken. We no longer carry this weight; in the name of all that is holy and good I am blessed with new light.

Now repeat the same prayer and invocation for your grandparents, your great grandparents and your great, great grandparents, going back as far as the previous 7 generations.

Angelic Healing

You are never alone – and I mean it! If you knew who walked by your side at all times, you would never be afraid.

Angels are messengers of Light. They are not specific to any one religion, nor do they have egos. Angels are a part of a higher spiritual order, and act as guardians of humanity. They are co-creators and helpers in any process that leads to your highest good and understanding. You might think of them as your personal spiritual assistants.

There are many types of angels on different levels, or triads, of creation, so to speak. Some of you may have some resistance to the word 'Angel' because of a particular religious association, but I would ask you to open your mind to what it actually means. You might instead liken an Angel to an archetype that exists to serve and help us in our becoming.

The Greeks used deities to act as spiritual archetypes representing particular virtues, values or intentions (and also flaws), and there is nothing wrong with personifying values into a way that serves a deeper meaning. From a purely energetic level and without any attachment to what really is and what really isn't, let me break it down for you: angels are representative of powerful frequencies.

These are very real energies that exist and operate on behalf of humanity beyond time and space as we currently understand it. When you invite the angelic realm into your life, you invite the miraculous. Some people experience angels as energetic forms of colour and light, while others may experience visions of winged beings with halos. One thing I can tell you for sure is that angels are real. I could not heal without their assistance.

Angels have specific duties and unique areas of expertise that may lend themselves to certain aspects of life. By calling on these assistants, we call upon illumination, energetic support and love to help us find our way. They help us clear energy and aid the manifestation process.

The thing about working with angels is that you have to ask for their help. They will not intervene without your permission:

Ask the Light and the Light will come.

Set an intention to receive wisdom that is for your highest good, and you will.

Nourish the relationship and it will nourish you.

What you appreciate, appreciates.

How can you expect Light to serve you if you do not serve it?

The act of asking for help, in itself, speaks of courage. Being open to receive that help speaks of trust. Whether it's a long day at the office, a family tragedy, a break-up, or a physical illness – evoking angelic energy through intention, prayer and gratitude brings healing and peace to the moment.

Here is a list of Archangels to call upon in times of need.

- **ARCHANGEL ANIEL:** 'Grace of God', helps you return to grace and your divine essence, aligned with the stars and the Moon (a great angel to evoke for Moon rituals, see page 136).

- **ARCHANGEL ARIEL:** 'Lioness of God', bravery, focus, courage, elegant movements, boosting confidence, divine magic, manifestation, animals.

- **ARCHANGEL AZRIEL:** 'Whom God Helps', animals, environmental concerns, grief, death.

- **ARCHANGEL GABRIEL:** 'Messenger of God', writing, speaking, communication with teachers, throat chakra, the arts, mothers, children, parenting.

- **ARCHANGEL HANIEL:** 'Glory of God', uses Moon energy to aid with miraculous shifts, helps you to live to your highest potential, polish your skills, magical, nurturing.

- **ARCHANGEL JEREMIEL:** 'Mercy of God', in difficult times call on him to deliver mercy to all involved, to develop more merciful outlook, respect for self and others, assists life review when we cross over.

- **ARCHANGEL JOPHIEL:** 'Beauty of God', beauty in all forms, spring cleaning, feng shui angel, helps to beautify relationships, environments or life itself.

- **ARCHANGEL METATRON:** Chief angel to Tree of Life, Enoch, overseer of highly sensitive, psychic or empathic children, time bender, shape shifter, sacred geometry.

- **ARCHANGEL MICHAEL:** 'He Who Is Like God', cuts negativity, for courage, protection, warrior energy with sword of light cutting through blocks, love, power, strength, faith.

- **ARCHANGEL RAGUEL:** 'Friend of God', healing relationships, softens heart with forgiveness, harmony, order, cooperation, kindness, wisdom, fairness.

- **ARCHANGEL RAPHAEL:** 'Heals with God', supreme healer in the angelic realm, personal healing, healing careers, divine guidance.

- **ARCHANGEL RAZIEL:** 'Secrets of God', delivers esoteric wisdom of Spirit, ancient secrets, alchemy, works with spiritual teachers and students (you could liken him to the archetype Merlin).

- **ARCHANGEL SAMUEL**: 'God Sees', finder of lost items, helps when lost, or to find a career, love, global peace.

- **ARCHANGEL SANDALPHON**: 'Together with God', helps children, artists, musicians, actors, writers, anyone in the arts, prophecy, healing, manifestation, awakening.

- **ARCHANGEL SARIEL**: 'Prayer of God', helps people connect to Spirit through prayer, helps those who need focus and concentration, motivates people to share their truth with the Universe.

- **ARCHANGEL URIEL**: 'Light of God', fire or flame of God, healing life through the mental planes, psychic release, unblocks negative thought forms, ability to enlighten mind.

- **ARCHANGEL ZADKIEL**: 'Righteousness of God', helps transitions from one aspect to another, spiritual professor, helps human memory function, releases forgiveness, heals in dreams.

As I've mentioned, I am an angelic healer and work with angels all day every day. I call on them before working with clients, as I rise, upon meditation, when clearing my own energy and before I go to bed. I've even taught my daughter to do the same thing! The Archangels are my tribe. You too have guardian angels waiting to assist you, if you only open your heart to their guidance.

EVOKING THE ARCHANGELS

- Begin by meditating quietly for a few minutes.

- Surround yourself with a bubble filled with the light of love.

- Connect to the Earth and ground your energies; the quieter you are the better you will observe.

- Say this prayer:

    I call in the guidance that is here for my highest good and will help to elevate my consciousness. I ask that there be protection from any energies that would not be right for me.

    I wish to work for alignments that are good for my body and mind and emotions.

    I invite those being(s) which work for the highest consciousness and that will hold the highest vibration of love.

- Mentally evoke each Archangel by saying the name out loud or silently to yourself. See them surrounding you in a pillar of light, starting with:

Archangel Michael	Archangel Jophiel
Archangel Raphael	Archangel Metatron
Archangel Aniel	Archangel Raguel
Archangel Ariel	Archangel Raziel
Archangel Azriel	Archangel Sandalphon
Archangel Samuel	Archangel Sariel
Archangel Gabriel	Archangel Uriel
Archangel Haniel	Archangel Zadkiel
Archangel Jeremiel	

- Envision yourself receiving love, guidance and joy in this pillar of light for as long as you like.

- Hold gratitude for the experience and meditate for 2 to 3 minutes when you have completed the exercise.

CUTTING CORDS WITH ARCHANGEL MICHAEL

As I mentioned, the angels can help us clear our energy and I call on them before working on myself and my clients. Sometimes, people come to my office distressed over a conflict with another person and I can easily see how it is affecting their sense of personal power, which in turn distorts their energy flow.

Cords of attachment are created when our energy fields become entangled with those of other people due to charged, unresolved conflicts or power struggles that have resulted in sadness, anger, fear, resentment and guilt. Essentially, harsh emotions towards others creates energetic bonds with them.

Whether you're dealing with an overbearing mother-in-law, a load of exhausting, ego-based corporate politics or losing a lover, you have the power to disentangle and reclaim your energy and rise above the situation. To help you do so, try this exercise at home. It is a simple visualisation that will take just a few minutes.

- Imagine you are sitting in the heart of a beautiful rose on the top of a mountain. At first, all you can see is the vast expanse of nature and the sky around you.

- Now imagine the person with whom you have issues is sitting in a rose on a mountain across from you, and you are looking at one another.

- Imagine the other person surrounded in a sphere of Light and send a beam of compassion to them. It doesn't matter if your personality despises this person. Rise above yourself and send them some Light.

- Call in legions of angels to surround the other person.

- Call on Archangel Michael who holds a mighty sword of truth and stands at the right hand of Source/Light/God.

- See the cord of energy that connects the two of you.

- See Archangel Michael flying down and cutting that cord with his sword as the angels on the opposite mountain lift the other person into the upper ethers in the sphere of Light.

- Bless them.

- Imagine Archangel Michael vacuuming up any debris or density from your field with a blue tube of light.

- Open your eyes when you feel complete with the visualisation. Thank any and all energies that assisted in uplifting your spirit.

3. SUPERCHARGE YOUR LIFE

You now know a little bit more about who you truly are as a being of light. You may already be walking a little taller as you strut down the street. It's time to take a look at how you can enhance your healing path by implementing everyday powerful tools such as meditation, prayer, affirmations and other manifestation techniques to supercharge your life. The areas addressed here serve to upgrade and enrich your world – no matter which paths you choose to take.

HIGH-VIBE HEROES

A high-vibrational lifestyle is imbued with enchantment, synchronicity, dedication, power and energy. It is rich and fulfilling; and tranquillity, health, compassion, freedom and wisdom will come when we live consistently in such a way.

New human archetypes with pioneering vision are emerging as our paradigm shifts and our consciousness evolves to meet the demands of these times. This new age is giving rise to people with access to greater awareness and higher sensitivity levels. Evolution creates new iterations of power. But we have to decide what this means as we continue to mix, match, merge and develop new ideas while the world shifts. As we evolve and grow, harnessing inner power becomes an important choice we all must make.

The kinds of role models needed at this time are those who promote individual and collective empowerment through their thoughts, words and deeds. At home, work or out with friends, they live and create with a higher purpose in mind. Instead of keeping that higher purpose on a shelf and taking it down to use during 'spiritual moments', these ideologies paint the lens of the higher mind. Their higher purpose becomes like a beautiful stained-glass window, allowing virtue to colour and illuminate each moment of the day. They encourage others to be the best versions of themselves, as they lead by example.

As Einstein once said, 'A new type of thinking is essential if mankind is to survive and move toward higher levels.' On that note, I invite you to do whatever it takes for you to rise. If you use your intuition, you'll have a better idea of how that applies to you. Surviving and moving towards higher levels means, in today's world, thriving and expanding your consciousness. When we do so, we teach without having to say a word.

Authenticity is the new enlightenment. To be authentic you have to truly know who you are. When you do know that deepest part of yourself and let it guide your path, your ideas about leadership, priorities and how you spend your time and energy may begin to change.

We are the ones that must decide what role models look like for our children. I call on those who know they can be real-deal powerhouses, bearing the torch of true leadership in whatever ways they can, big or small. We all have roles to play. And each one is important.

Anyone can be a role model for the times – you don't need money, a great body, fame, followers or the perfect downward dog position on your yoga mat. By tuning in to your energy, maintaining an aligned and powerful self-care practice that works for you, prioritising virtue of character, committing to not only serving yourself but others, you can unlock your true potential. Healing and working with your energy will help you embody those ideals. Moreover, adopting practices like meditation, prayer, affirmation, gratitude and manifestation techniques will help supercharge your entire life.

It takes real strength to use your powers intentionally, and for good. The time to do so is now.

What is Real Strength?

- A deep sense of self love.

- Generosity.

- Dedication to a personal growth practice.

- Integrity.

- Living with intention in all areas of your life.

- Being bold enough to take risks.

- Being true to yourself.

- Taking care of yourself emotionally, physically, spiritually, financially and mentally.

- Having healthy boundaries.

- Leading by example, not from a rulebook.

- Choosing to envision the best possible outcome for yourself, others and the world, despite the odds.

- Facing your past and pain to heal your wounds.

- Giving yourself permission to do what your intuition guides you to do.

- Doing whatever it takes to balance your family life, work, relationships and rest.

- Changing when it's time to change things.

- Being an active listener.

- Saying NO to forces that drain your energy. Taking active steps towards your goals.

- Reading between the lines.

- Committing to being an eternal student.

- Having grit.

- Knowing the difference between false power and real power.

- Practising neutrality and compassion.

- Accepting that you are perfect, right now, already, in this moment, reading this book – and believing it.

MEDITATION

Meditation is the art and science of training the mind. It is the gateway to awakening. Awakening does not have to be your goal when establishing a regular meditation practice, although it may be an accidental effect. Lucky you! But what is awakening? It has been called many names; however, here I will describe it as freedom from suffering – and not just in momentary glimpses of enlightenment. It is the mature actualisation of joy and peace in the form of sustained tranquillity and equanimity, which are just two of the benefits of meditation. Higher insight, awareness, health, intelligence, focus, serenity and freedom are also available to you through dedicated meditation practice.

You cannot fully tap into your intuitive power or harness the Light within without cultivating stillness and a neutral mind. Meditation helps you do just that. It also helps us to release subconscious fears and negative habits, and to develop inner stability and focus. Focus is required so that you can direct your energy with unfailing intention. Meditation is a massive part of supercharging your life and I would say one of the most important, relevant and practical takeaways from this book. If nothing else, meditate!

The continuous experience of a meditative state is known as *Simran* in the yogic world. It is a state in which life is experienced as a constant spiritual flow, a blissfully creative and peaceful feeling. This state is the goal. But not having a goal is how you achieve this state! Ha!

For those who wish to purify the mind and know the unknown, meditation is the key. Despite all the self-study, trainings, mentors, listening and learning, I am going to let you in on a little secret …

MEDITATION IS MY GREATEST TEACHER.

MEDITATION IS HOW I RECEIVED THE MOST PROFOUND WISDOM OF MY LIFE.

MEDITATION GIFTED ME DIRECT COMMUNION WITH SPIRIT.

And it is my belief that direct communion with Spirit (i.e. the Source) is the answer to every problem you will ever face. Yes, that is a banger of a statement. And, yes, I stand by it.

The first time I tried to meditate I was 8 years old. I didn't know what mediation was. One day, I remember staring into the flames in the fire when no one else was around. It calmed me.

I did not grow up in a household where meditation practices were the norm. I just knew that sitting quietly by the fire, gradually closing my eyes and sitting in a comfortable, cross-legged position with a straight spine made me feel really good. After I found my position, I started to chant 'OHM' (a Hindu mantra and vibration) without knowing what it means. To this day, meditating in front of fire is my favourite way to tap into higher states of consciousness.

Direct experience offers insight. Insight is known in some Buddhist traditions as 'Vipassana', a term also used to describe a particular style of meditation. When Vipassana is combined with a tranquil state of being, or 'Samatha', a doorway to the experience of direct communion with higher consciousness is made available. There are many approaches to meditation and many variations of those approaches. The Samatha-Vipassana approach is very old and – as the name suggests – means, 'the practice of tranquillity and insight'. Other terms you may hear when researching Buddhist meditation might include 'Samadhi', which means using intense stable attention, and 'Sati', which means mindfulness.

A wonderful reference and guide for the modern meditator is *The Mind Illuminated*. It offers a step-by step-approach for the beginner or well-practised meditator. John Yates PhD, or

Culadasa as he is known to his students, is a globally respected meditation master with decades of experience in Tibetan and Theravadin Buddhist traditions. He has taught neuroscience and physiology at a university level and his approach to teaching meditation is structural, with cumulative steps combining neuroscience and many Buddhist traditions.

There are many types of meditation and only you can determine the one with the most resonance for you. Some are structured and organised with sequences, while others are less rigid. The issue for the modern Westerner is that these ancient systems for understanding meditation are not readily accessible because the antiquated language does not resonate with our understandings. Ancient, sacred scripture can be a little difficult to get your head around. This is why finding a teacher master, or a structured form of education through older books, recorded lectures, schools or training programs is usually quite helpful. Some Tibetan meditations are rich with guidance. Many find that using guided meditations can be helpful because the instruction assists their mind's focus in the beginning. For those with a more empathetic or artistic nature, sound combined with guided instruction in a meditation might be a great place to start. For the more analytical or scientific mind, the study and practice of an ancient system combined with an intellectual dive into the scientific benefits may be more suitable. Again, knowing yourself will help you discern what will work for you. So be willing to try different methods.

Shunryu Suzuki Roshi is a monk who brought Zen teachings to the West and helped them spread. His book *Zen Mind, Beginner's Mind: Informal Talks on Zen Meditation and Practice* is a compelling resource for understanding meditation and Eastern philosophy as related to Zen teachings and Mahayana Buddhism, which focuses on the teachings found in the Mahayana Sutras. In the prologue of *Zen Mind, Beginner's Mind*, he wrote: 'In the beginner's mind there are many possibilities, in the expert's mind there are few'. The profound becomes more obvious with a pure mind. Zen practices, among other forms of Buddhism, are intended to keep the mind pure.

Transcendental Meditation, or TM, is a meditation technique brought to the West by Maharishi Mahesh Yogi over 50 years ago and is used by millions of people worldwide. It is said to be an effortless form of meditation and is very popular in the West. It incorporates mantras and is designed to be practised by the student of this technique for 15 to 20 minutes, twice a day. There is usually a nominal fee for learning the technique, which varies from country to country.

Kundalini yoga mantras use ancient Sanskrit phrases that hold vibration and meaning, and which are repeated continuously in song, mentally or in a chant. They both clear out the subconscious and invite your being to embody the energy of the mantra as you continue to repeat the phrase.

Some styles of meditation simply follow the breath and ask that you are present and focused on your inner and outer surroundings without running off with your thoughts. Wayne Dyer, author and spiritual teacher, described meditation as 'floating in the gap between thoughts'.

Getting Started with Meditation

- Establish a meditation practice: be consistent and diligent. This means sticking to it every single day and devoting yourself wholeheartedly to your practice instead of daydreaming or looking at cushions online and calling it meditation.

- Set goals: for example, overcoming impatience, distraction and boredom. Choose to do it for 21 or 40 days in a row, like setting yourself a challenge in yoga.

- Keep your attention on your breath: this means neutrally observing the subtle sensations experienced from breathing deeply and slowly.

- Create an altar or sacred space: having a place in your home that is devoted to stillness sets an intentional, energetic tone and it is more inviting when the time comes to meditate.

- Know that with enough practice, deeper communion with your highest self is absolutely possible.

- Don't quit because it's hard. That's like saying you don't work out because you get out of breath.

- You get what you give: like anything else, what you appreciate, appreciates.

The Relaxation Response

The relaxation response (a term coined by Dr Herbert Benson and popularised in his book of the same name) is a state of decreased activity for muscles and organs that reduces the respiratory rate and metabolism as well as heart and brain activity. It is essentially the opposite of the fight-or-flight response. He wrote his book about it based on his study of meditation and the mind–body connection. The relaxation response, which describes the state that occurs in meditation, can be achieved by implementing these conditions, according to Benson:

- A quiet environment.

- A mental device such as a repeated word or phrase (for example, saying the word *love* over and over).

- The adoption of a passive attitude.

- A comfortable position.

- Practise for 10 to 20 minutes, 2 times a day.

AFFIRMATIONS

An affirmation is a statement of intent using positive language.
For example, if you are facing an illness, a strong affirmation to
use would be: *I am in perfect health.*

Most minds would start to worry about their disease, mentally
saying: *Oh I don't want to be sick. I am uncomfortable. Please,
Universe, take this away from me. I can't take it anymore.* In
thought forms and words like these, all the person is doing
is giving their energy to what they DO NOT want, which is
ultimately counterproductive. Remember:

Energy goes where attention flows.

We have to commit to the conditions we seek to produce,
instead of being upset about what we do not have. Ideally,
we can hold space for what is without judgement, while also
deciding to hold the knowing, with gratitude, that life is bringing
us even greater good.

Affirmations help us to speed up the process of bringing about
the desired results by training our minds, emotions and energy
to be ready and willing to receive them. However, we have
to understand that it takes time to rewire our neural pathways,

especially when patterns have been ingrained for long periods of time or instituted in childhood. In fact, our adult operating system is usually running on childhood programming formulated in the ages of 0 to 7. Whatever was going on then may be affecting how you think, speak, feel and operate now.

So how do we change the way we think? By impressing new thought patterns on our subconscious mind. For our purposes here, imagine your mind as being divided in two parts: the conscious mind and the subconscious mind. That the mind is divided into two aspects is not a new concept. In Balinese traditions the conscious, *sekala*, and subconscious, *niskala*, are both discussed in regards to healing. The conscious mind contains the thoughts we have all day – that pop up, then go away. The subconscious mind is always at work, when you are asleep and awake. It tells your lungs to breathe and your heart to beat. It is intelligent and powerful, but the thing is – it takes orders from you.

Joseph Murphy PhD explains these two parts of the mind in his book *The Power of The Subconscious Mind* as being like the ship's captain (conscious mind) and the crew that keep the engine going (subconscious mind). The crew take orders, they are trained to obey the captain. So, if you are telling yourself,

'I'll never make it. I will never be enough. I suck at life. Why even try...' and so on, your subconscious mind will be like, 'All right guys, s/he sucks at life, let's go ahead and affirm her command by making things even suckier! We are such good subordinates!'

The Hocus Pocus is Focus

I've now made affirmations a part of my everyday life and custom-tailor them to what I need at the moment. I have a list of affirmations that help me to get through challenging times and moments of personal growth that require more self-care and attention than usual. These include:

Thank you, God, for helping me get out of my own way, so I can show others what is truly possible.

I am safe.

I am cherished.

I am valuable.

My creative potential is infinite.

I am perfect health.

I am good fortune.

I am free, inspired and glowing with Source Light.

I am grateful for everything I have. I have everything I need. My needs are perfectly met right here and now.

The things I tell my subconscious mind evolve as necessary; you don't have to use the same affirmation for 10 years. Once your brain gets it and it becomes an ingrained belief, it's on to the next issue. You can work with multiple affirmations at one time; however, I would suggest focusing on just a couple of life areas in any given period so as not to spread your energies and intentions too thin.

The more often the conscious mind reinforces a belief, the more that belief's energy pattern is reinforced in the subconscious mind and your energy matches its vibrational output.

Here's the thing though — what happens when you don't believe what you are saying to yourself?

Inner conflict.

And what happens when we experience inner conflict?

Feelings of disharmony.

If used inappropriately or at the wrong time, positive affirmations can be a disservice to your state of being. If your vibrational output is at odds with your mental narrative, inner conflict is created – and will attract the like.

Affirmations only work when they parallel the energy you are putting out and how you truly feel. If you're feeling down, wait until you are in a state of neutrality before working to retrain your subconscious. You want to work with the mind in a vibrational state of belief, openness and willingness. If your affirmations come from a place of desperation, they carry the energy of fear with them.

Of course, 'faking it till you make it' can sometimes work. I am simply suggesting that you are strategic about when and how you incorporate affirmations into your life. For example, if something really bad happens that upsets you, take some time to nurture yourself back to neutral or at least find a chilled-out space before using affirmations. Do this by doing things that relax you: read a book, watch a movie, take a walk, play with your kids, clear your mind of the upsetting thing or just focus on the present moment. Shoot for calm and fun.

It is important to mention that we should avoid creating a spiritual bypass or using spiritual ideas to justify harmful behaviours; and we can achieve this by dismantling deflective tendencies and honouring all aspects of our emotional selves. This requires facing and processing pain in an honest, healthy way. Processing painful emotions and events does not mean overindulging in negativity. There is a fine line here and discernment is required. The more you hold space for the truth of your experience, good or bad, the easier it gets to use that discernment successfully. My point is, using affirmations is not an excuse to avoid uncomfortable inner work or facing your pain. But once you find yourself in a neutral state of mind again, work with the life-enhancing, self-honouring words you've crafted as your affirmations. If you are already joyful and feeling the vibes – even better. Milk it. Affirm your face off and rewire that subconscious mind all night long!

Affirmations are similar to mantras in that they are both repetitive, positive and are used to train the mind. And, as I've mentioned, a focused and peaceful mind can direct your energy and intentions.

THINK BEYOND THE
LIMITATIONS OF YOUR LIFE

PRAYER

Meditation is listening to Spirit.
Prayer is talking to Spirit.

In the context of energy healing, prayer means using words to focus your intention and speaking to the Source of your energy. I use both affirmative language and gratitude when praying.

Not only your thoughts, but your words, speech and moods create a vibrational output that sends a message to the Universe around you. So how can we use our words and thoughts to amplify the message and get back our desired outcome?

Again, like affirmations, the person who prays from a place of desperation and fear will likely have a very different outcome than a person who prays from a place of gratitude. For example, let's say you're low on cash and the rent is due in days. This is hugely stressful. You are incredibly worried. You might turn to prayer, not sure what else to do, uttering words like: *Please, God/Universe, I only need enough to get by. I'm not asking for much. I know we haven't really jammed in a while but I'll do anything if you help me out, God/Universe...*

Being desperate for crumbs is not the kind of consciousness that lends itself to the belief that the Universe will support you – and that, indeed, it does so by design. This approach does not lend itself to the belief that there is enough for everyone, even you. In the mind of Source, abundance reigns. When we tap into that current, abundance flows unto us. However, in this scenario, the person is going against the natural order of the Source by believing in lack and supporting scarcity instead. A prayer that speaks to trust and faith would work a bit better.

Or, imagine you are a parent and your toddler is screaming in a high chair, eyes bugging, snot dripping, high-pitched squealing at the top of his lungs. You know something is wrong and have no idea how to help. You may try all sorts of things – wiping his nose, changing a nappy, burping, a lullaby, milk, food – nothing is working. If only he could calm down and point to the toy he dropped on the floor! Then, you'd know exactly what he needs to get back to happy. Just as the mother cannot understand her distressed child, Spirit cannot understand your call for help as clearly as you might wish if you are in a state of distress.

Chaotic disturbances cloud us in denser vibrations and the associated heavy emotions muddle our aura. It becomes harder for Source to hear what we need. Instead of clarity, we put out noise and static. So try to get into the habit of communicating

your needs regularly on good days as much as bad days.
And do so clearly.

That does not mean it isn't OK to pray or speak to Source in
desperate moments. I do so all the time. I'm human. But I know
that it works a lot better when I am calm, clear and direct – just
like any form of communication.

There's a Reason for Everything

Remember that things usually happen for a reason. I've
been through the wringer about a million times, yet have
never experienced a moment of perceived loss that didn't
lead to the opening of a new opportunity.

In those moments of perceived loss, don't try to hold
on to what you're losing. Trust that something better is
coming your way.

Let go of everything. See what stays.

Make a Prayer

An ideally worded prayer for someone seeking more love, intimacy and connection in their life might go something like this:

Dear [insert your chosen word here, such as God/Spirit/ Source],

Thank you for looking after me. Thank you for your support.

I am easily able to be at peace with the conditions in my life. I trust in [Spirit's] infinite knowledge and divine plan.

Avalanches of love circulate through every area of my life. I give love generously. I receive love abundantly. I use this abundance of love to express my divine gifts to the world, to support myself and inspire others.

I fall asleep relaxed, in peace and in the comfort of [God's] love. I know that I am love and love finds me, always.

Thank you, [Spirit], for this knowing.

Amen.

Take control of your life in your prayer and celebrate the good things, as well as asking for what you need.

MANIFESTATION

Manifesting opportunity is not so much about what you specifically do; instead, it is more about who you become as a result of what you do, think, say, feel and vibrate, etc. Your becoming is your vibrational output. And your vibration will call in matching aspects. Creating a detailed outline that specifies the exact things you'd like to see appear in your life is one way of focusing your intention. And I support other actions that do so too, so long as you drop any energy relating to control, entitlement or desperation around what you are seeking.

Don't worry about getting what you want. Focus on who you want to be in this world. The more often you strengthen your connection to Spirit, the more often Spirit will connect with you through opportunity and positive manifestations. The Light will begin talking to you through signs and signals. It feels like magic, but it has nothing to do with magic: the signs are normal, natural and happening everyday if you are tuned in to spot them.

Life is meant to be an effortless expression of joy. It is meant to feel good. When we embark upon the spiritual path of awakening there may be initiations and pitfalls, challenges and obstacles to overcome. But, deep inside, those of us who hear the call to truth take those steps towards alignment with courage, knowing that it is the only true way forwards.

The truth is, you can't really veer off your path. All rivers lead to the ocean. However, you can make the journey a hell of a lot more difficult than it needs to be (take it from someone who is stubborn!).

The more sensitive you are to an awareness of your energy alignment, the easier it is to tell if you are out of your flow. That means the more often you feel connected to Source and your own glowing, balanced energy, the more quickly you will know when something is off. The Universe always gives us signs when we are on the right track. And when something feels off – guess what? It usually is. Sad news and suffering happen to the best of us for the purposes of growth and learning, but along the way, Spirit will give us signs to help us avoid unnecessary pain.

All we need to do is follow the path with heart.

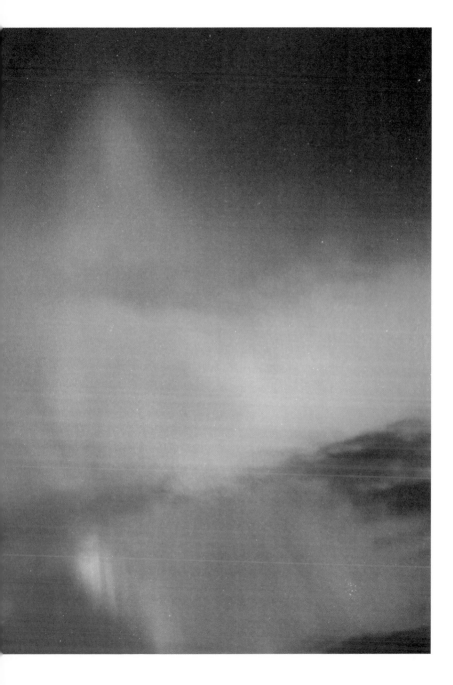

10 Signs you are Living in Divine Flow

1. SYNCHRONICITIES OCCUR REGULARLY

You find money in your jean pockets exactly when you need it. You are in the right place at the right time to meet that perfect person who can help you in your career. Friends call just when you are thinking about them. You fondly recall your favourite uncle who passed away – and three days later are asked out by a dude with the same first and middle name as him.

Signs show up all the time through number sequences, the media and the natural world. Things just seem to fall in place. At first, it's trippy! Eventually, it becomes the norm.

2. YOU FEEL EXPANSION AND EASE AROUND THE PEOPLE CLOSEST TO YOU

You've got to a place where your best friends really *are* your best friends. You only tolerate those who truly see you and uplift you. In your work life or personal life, the people who are drawn into your sphere of influence are basically awesome.

3. WORK DOESN'T FEEL LIKE WORK

You do not wake up and curse your alarm on Monday mornings. In fact, work feels so playful and joyful that you are not even aware of when it's a weekend versus a weekday! Now, no one likes to go over their accounts or pay their taxes (well, maybe some people), but in general your work is your passion and your passion is your work. It lights you up. You are really good at it. You could talk about it for hours.

You've made clear decisions and taken active steps to follow your dreams. When you show up for work or professional engagements, it is with excitement and a genuine appreciation for the ability to share your gifts to the world. And when someone asks, 'What would you be doing if you had 10 million dollars?', your response is, 'Exactly what I am doing right now.' #boom

4. SELF-CARE BECOMES AN EFFORTLESS PRIORITY

You want to eat well because it feels good. You want to work out because your body wants to move and feel grounded on the physical plane. Weight seems to fall off without you even trying, because you've let go of emotional baggage. You aren't interested in going out to party all night because you're really excited about your 8 a.m. workout the next day.

You know that investing in yourself is the best investment you can make, so you budget for healing sessions and relaxation experiences. You tell your friends to catch you at the library because expanding your mind is more important than getting more followers on Instagram.

You are OK with stillness, with solitude. Meditation becomes more reliable than external numbing agents. You give yourself permission to cancel plans with friends occasionally, because listening to your body when it needs rest takes priority over 'shoulds' that you don't really want to do. Food. Sleep. Exercise. Energy healing. Prayer. Meditation. Rest. Joy. Compassion. They all become your tools to be the best person you can be.

5. YOU SLEEP AT NIGHT

Health and hormones willing, when the heart is at rest, you will find peaceful sleep. Regular sleep was an issue for a lot of my life. It wasn't really until I found deep, deep peace that I could let down my guard fully in order to sleep. I worked with the following affirmations:

> I am willing to rest on Earth. Earth is a safe place.
>
> I am willing to be at peace. I am peace.
>
> I am willing to be supported. I am supported.
>
> My soul is at rest.

This kind of language can be very helpful for moving towards states of serenity.

You've let go of all the ways you've learned to protect yourself because you realise you are unbreakable. You no longer have any need to protect yourself and instead, you choose to open yourself.

You've taken measures to get off your digital devices at least an hour before bed, eat dinner early and attain a peaceful state before heading off to bed (all self-care practices).

You trust the Universe to have your back so you can rest.

6. SAYING 'NO' BECOMES EASY

Sayonara, 'shoulds'! Peace out 'obligatory appearances'. If it doesn't work for you, if you do not feel like giving your time or energy to it, you simply say no. You are neutral and polite in communication and you know that when you stay true to what works for you, everybody wins. You do not fear to make other people feel sad through your response because you know trying to manipulate the emotional responses of others by dishonouring your truth or 'people-pleasing' is ultimately a form of controlling energy. And you know that controlling energy diffuses your ability to manifest.

7. YOU SMILE THROUGHOUT THE DAY

You are perfectly delighted to watch how the wind makes the oak trees dance when the sparrow flits through them. You naturally take note of small, sweet things and the poetry of life. Your thoughts are on the goodness within you, without you and all that is coming to you. You are joyful. You don't even think about it. You just smile because it feels good.

8. YOU ARE EAGER AND EXCITED ABOUT THE FUTURE

Not only do you feel good things, but you anticipate and get excited like a small child about all the wonderful things you *know* are coming your way. Life moves from soldiering through a chaotic war zone, to being a kid with a million pounds in a sweet shop, choosing what sweet thing you get to have next! You are motivated because you are excited.

9. PEOPLE ARE DRAWN TO YOUR MAGNETISM

You're funny. Everybody at the party is laughing at your jokes. Your wit and cleverness are increasing and you aren't even trying. Why? You are flowing with Source energy and everything is smooth, baby. You live as a pure channel so your swagger is divine. People want to hear what you have to say and actively listen when you speak.

People come out of the woodwork and want to help you with projects or ambitions, just because they believe in you. You are invited to fun happenings. You feel supported because your soul tribe is flocking to you like a magnet. You've finally raised the authentic joy flag and those who are truly meant to be with you suddenly are.

10. MIRACULOUS OPPORTUNITY BECOMES THE NORM

Life dreams are suddenly available for the taking. You start receiving calls or emails from big shots or key people who support your work. You meet your divine romantic partner. Large sums of money come in. A friend offers to take you on a trip. The stars align! And by this time... you don't even question it. You know you've done enough inner work to create space for freedom and joy. You know that you ARE the master. Abundance is your birth right. Royalty is innate. And miracles are simply a way of life.

Now that you understand how you can feel in divine flow, let's talk about an important fundamental principle in regards to manifestation:

When you need nothing, you attract everything.

Every morning when you wake up, you have exactly everything you need to get through the day!

Project the Vision you Want to See

It is really common for people to cut out pictures of things they want and glue them onto a vision board, strategically placing the board where they can see it every day – with photos of beautiful homes, fancy cars, clothes, jewels, holidays and weddings, etc. That's totally cool. Again, it focuses your intentions. But don't expect that sh*t to magically appear without the consciousness to support it.

Vision boards won't generate the real-deal magnetic force that draws in conditions that make life joyous. Your consciousness is what will create and manifest your reality.

Real Power is Invisible

Now that we understand it is not about the method of manifesting but the energy behind it, the person who becomes it, the source that houses it – we can talk about a few aspects that make manifesting easier in the practical everyday sense.

The stuff that you want 'lightly' will come easily. When we have a sense of ease, we approach the world with the eyes of the child. With this light attitude, you are telling God/Source/Light, 'I know I am OK, no matter what. I am bountiful and happy. I would like this to happen, but I am more focused on my inner peace'. From a vibrational perspective, the Universe responds to the combination of your focused desire and your emotional state of wellbeing. Now, that combination is a high-vibe recipe for manifestation!

Often our desires, no matter how much we affirm, pray, plead and want, are accompanied by an overemphasis that leads to heaviness and ultimately resistance. The root of that overemphasis is the fear that we will not receive our heart's desire, so we affirm and pray and want and overemphasise more and more. In this way, we have a tendency to block our own manifestation process because we are adding fearful energy to the desire, instead of the peaceful, playful energy of abundance.

As we have seen, the Universe responds to your vibration – the core energy that you emit into the ether; not to what you say, nor what you pretend to be. So, when you find yourself wanting something but sense there is resistance associated with that desire, try taking these steps:

1. STOP THINKING.

Tune in to your energy and find your sense of ease. Go read a book under an oak tree. Engage in a hobby. Watch your favourite movie, focus on your positive friendships – all the good stuff. Leave the desire be until you come back to a sense of ease. The daily practice of writing down in a notebook all the things for which you are grateful is very helpful.

2. MEDITATE.

When you feel at ease, quiet your mind. You cannot manifest without focused intention. Meditation causes us to take a step back and gain a greater perspective on what is really important in this world. Build your inner power and enhance that sense of ease through meditation.

3. FOCUS.

Only when you are calm and centred should you pray, affirm and apply carefully selected thoughts to your desire. Maintain a sense of detachment. Maintain that sense of ease. After meditation, spend 5 to 10 minutes each day focusing on your desire with this relaxed attitude.

4. LET IT GO.

To try to take control is to block your energy – believe me, I know! Send your desire to the sky. Give it to the birds. Letting go requires trust. Look at your relationship with yourself and this world. Is the world good or bad? Are people out to get you, or are they helpful?

Your ability to let go directly relates to your core belief about whether this world is a safe place to thrive. What is so cool about letting go is that you get to choose whether or not you want to trust this life process. But I promise you, things work out a lot more smoothly when you do. Letting go is about surrender and trust. It's what high-vibe heroes do.

CONCLUSION

We all want to live an illuminated life. We all want the big joy. We want to surprise ourselves and others with our creations and our works. We need to learn how to dig deep to do that. And we need to know where to look.

All the understandings, systems and teachings described in these pages – which have thrived for eons – are signs and pathways that humanity was made to better itself. You are a unique being. You are creating thoughts and opportunities that have never been done quite like you do it in the entire history of humanity. We should celebrate this.

It is my hope that this introduction to various forms of energy systems, healing processes and higher ideals will serve to help you plant your own seeds of light and grow them into something auspicious, surprising and shocking that changes all of us.

There may be subjects in this book that you've never heard of before and there're so many areas to surrender to or experiment with in order to grow a profound life. Only you will know what is right for you. The healing path is non-linear and unique to your being. No one can tell you what is right or wrong for you. That is your job, boss!

We are all on this journey together, embracing the path of connection and unity. Sometimes we stumble. Sometimes we fall. But at the end of the day, it's simple. We all want to be more connected to each other, our humanness, our depth – and to something greater. I promise you, you already are. I promise you, it is there waiting for you.

With your head held high, you will walk tall, one foot in front of the other, through the darkness, beyond the light and into the truth. Un-f*ck-with-able and infinite, you are the keeper of grace on this planet. It is up to you to lead the way. I wish you luck and so much light on your journey.

May the Source be with you.

RESOURCES

Below are the details of a range of inspirational books and online resources. (However, these listings do not imply any endorsement by those mentioned of the material in this book.)

Further Reading

Andrews, Ted, *Animals-speak* (Llewellyn, 1994).

Anon, *A Course In Miracles* (Foundation for Inner Peace, 2008).

Babbitt, Edwin, *Principles of Light and Colour* (Kessinger, 1998).

Bhadantacariya Buddhaghosa, *Path of Purification* (Buddhist Publication Society, 1991).

Blakeway, Jill, *Energy Medicine* (Scribe, 2019).

Dalai Lama, *Stages of Meditation* (Snow Lion, 2013).

Davies, Olivia, *Meister Eckhart: Selected Writings*, trans. and ed. (Penguin, 1994).

Dyer, Wayne, *The Power Of Intention* (Hay House, 2004).

Grand, David, *Brainspotting* (Sounds True, 2013).

Khan, Inayat, *The Art Of Being and Becoming* (Omega, 1989).

King, Godfrey, *The I Am Discourses* (Atlantic, 1935).

Luk, A.D.K., *Law of Life: Book One and Two* (ADK Luk Publications, 1959).

Myss, Carolyn, *Defy Gravity* (Hay House, 2011).

Archetypes (Hay House, 2014).

Rumi, Jelaluddin, *The Essential Rumi*, ed. Coleman Barks (HarperCollins, 1995).

Singer, Michael, *The Untethered Soul* (New Harbinger, 2007).

Stevens, Jose and Lena, *The Power Path* (New World Library, 2002).

Suzuki, Shunryu, *Zen Mind, Beginner's Mind* (Shambhala, 2005).

Tolle, Eckhart, *The Power Of Now* (Yellow Kite, 2005).

A New Earth (Penguin, 2009).

Tzu, Lao, *Tao Te Ching*, trans. D. C. Lau (Penguin, 2000).

Virtue, Doreen, *Healing with the Angels* (Hay House, 1999).

Walsch, Neale Donald, *The Complete Conversations With God* (Perigee Books, 2005).

Weiss, Brian, *Messages From the Masters* (Piatkus, 2000).

Yates, John and Immergut, Matthew, *The Mind Illuminated* (Hay House, 2017).

Useful Addresses

Abraham-Hicks materials and teachings: www.abraham-hicks.com

Astrology with leading astrologer Sandy Sitron: www.sandysitron.com

Brainspotting with founder Dr David Grand: www.brainspotting.com

Breathwork with David Elliot: www.davidelliott.com

Breathwork with Erin Telford: erintelford.com

John Donohue, poet and philosopher: www.johnodonohue.com

Intuitive Energy Training with Russell Forsyth: www.russellforsyth.com

J. Krishmamurti, teachings and resources: https://kfoundation.org/

KRI Aquarian Teacher Training, as taught by Yogi Bhajan:
    www.kundaliniyoga.org.uk

Maori healing: www.maorihealers.com, www.terongopae.com,
    www.kawa-arika.maorihealers.com

Marcel Vogel information: www.vogelcrystals.net

Meditation with Eve Smith: www.sitwitheve.com

The Theosophical Society, teaching and resources:
    www.theosophical.org

Unlock Your Quantum Powers training with Dr Jean Houston:
    www.evolvingwisdom.com/jeanhouston/quantumpowers

Alan Watts talks and lectures: www.alanwatts.com

The Work method with Byron Katie: www.thework.com

INDEX

Note: page numbers in **bold** refer to illustrations.

ABOUT THE AUTHOR

Kalisa Augustine is an experienced holistic health practitioner, offering private classes and workshops in L.A. and New York. Kalisa's energy healing, energetic purification, soul coaching and vibrational therapies (including chromotherapy, crystal bowl sound healing and therapeutic-grade crystal healing) bring her clients greater happiness, peace, clarity and joy for life.

Kalisa has been featured on The Untitled Action Bronson Show, in *Vogue*, *Beauty Bets*, *Bustle*, *Buzzfeed*, *New York Times*, MindBodyGreen, *Vice*, Well + Good, HBFit, PopSugar, *Marie Claire*, *Domino*, The Numinous, The Free People Blog and *WMagazine*.

Find her at www.kalisaaugustine.com and on Instagram @kalisa_augustine